THE STAIRS

MUNICH PROJECTION

Curated by
Elisabeth Schweeger

PETER GREENAWAY

MERRELL HOLBERTON
PUBLISHERS LONDON

THE STAIRS

MÜNCHEN
PROJEKTIONEN

Kuratorin:
Elisabeth Schweeger

PETER GREENAWAY

MERRELL HOLBERTON
PUBLISHERS LONDON

VORWORT

Einer der weltweit renommiertesten Regisseure und Ausstellungsmacher, der Engländer Peter Greenaway, setzt mit seinem Projekt »Projection-Frames« in München analysierend und zugleich ironisierend den 100. Geburtstag des Kinos in Szene.

Während im gleichen Jahr am Berliner Reichstag Geschichte durch Verhüllung sichtbar gemacht wurde, entmaterialisiert Greenaway in einem weiteren Schritt das künstlerische Darstellungsmittel, indem er das gleiche Medium wählt, das wesentlich zur Wirkung der Filme beiträgt: Licht.

Die Gegenwart der Kunstform Film ist flüchtig, denn jede Sekunde eines Films wird mit seinem weiteren Abspulen nur noch zur Erinnerung an Vergangenes.

Wenn sich mit Einbruch der Nacht unsere Phantasie vermehrt für Wahrnehmungen öffnet, fangen die 100 Rahmen durch Reflexion von Lichtinstallationen Impressionen der Film- und Baugeschichte ein.

Vergangenheit und Architektur der Stadt verbinden sich dabei mit dem Erlebnishorizont des Betrachters.

Greenaways Konzept geht davon aus, daß die Filmgeschichte eng verbunden ist mit bestimmten Wahrnehmungsformen, die seit Jahrhunderten unser kulturelles Verständnis bestimmen.

Kino als visuell erfahrbare Kunst wird in Abhängigkeit vom technischen Fortschritt gezeigt, der im ersten Jahrhundert der Filmgeschichte fortschreitend neue Visualisierungsmöglichkeiten eröffnet hat und so auch auf unser Bewußtsein und unsere Erwartungen einwirkt.

Ebenso setzt sich die Ausstellung »Projection-Frames« mit der Vernetzung von Film, bildender Kunst und Architektur auseinander.

Angesichts seiner Tradition kann Bayern mit seiner Geschichte und seinen historischen Gebäuden einen interessanten Rahmen für die internationale Geburtstagsfeier bilden.

Möge sich die hundertjährige Geschichte des Kinos mit der baugeschichtlichen Vergangenheit des Freistaates Bayern zu einem gelungenen Kunstwerk verbinden.

Hans Zehetmair
Bayerischer Staatsminister für Unterricht, Kultus, Wissenschaft und Kunst
Stellvertretender Ministerpräsident

GELEITWORT ZUR AUSSTELLUNG

In diesem Jahr feiert der Film seinen 100. Geburtstag und eine Vielzahl von Veranstaltungen beschäftigen sich mit diesem Thema. Zu den sicher herausragenden Ereignissen zählt ein Projekt des englischen Filmemachers, Malers und Ausstellungskurators Peter Greenaway für München.

Der Künstler setzt hiermit seine Serie von 10 Ausstellungen unter dem Titel »Stairs« (Treppen) fort, die 1994 in Genf mit dem Thema 'Schauplätze' ihren Anfang genommen hat und in München (1995), Barcelona (1996) und weiteren Weltstädten bis zum Jahr 2000 fortgesetzt werden wird. Mit dieser anspruchsvollen Serie von Installationen unternimmt Greenaway den Versuch herauszufinden, ob nach den ersten hundert Jahren des Films die Erwartungen erfüllt wurden, die in die größte Kunstform des 20. Jahrhunderts gesetzt wurden. Allgemein gilt der Film als das kommunikativste Ausdrucksmittel des 20. Jahrhunderts.

Mit seinen Filmen, Opern und Ausstellungen vertritt Greenaway die These »Wir lernen Lesen und Schreiben, aber nicht Sehen«. Mit der Installationsreihe »Stairs«/»Projection-Frames«, die 1995 in München zu sehen sein wird, trägt er zu diesem »Wieder-Sehen-Lernen« bei.

Greenaway hat für seine Reflexion über den Film öffentliche Plätze und Gebäude gewählt, 100 Orte in der Stadt, an denen er 100 Projektionsflächen installieren wird.

Die komplexe Geschichte des Films soll so für eine größtmögliche Anzahl von Betrachtern aufbereitet werden.

München blickt als Kunststadt und Stadt des Films auf eine lange Tradition zurück. Diese Tradition muß neu belebt und mit neuen Inhalten besetzt werden. Ich freue mich daher besonders, daß die Landeshauptstadt München, die an »Stairs«/»Projection-Frames« als Veranstalter beteiligt ist, helfen konnte, dieses auch über München hinaus ausstrahlende Ereignis zu realisieren. Es trägt auf ungewöhnliche Art dazu bei, die Stadtgeschichte mit der Geschichte des Films zu verbinden, die Stadt mit neuen Augen zu sehen und ihren Ruf als Kulturstadt prospektiv in die Zukunft fortzuschreiben.

Christian Ude
Oberbürgermeister der Landeshauptstadt München

T

1002463306

ZUR ARBEIT MIT PETER GREENAWAY

Warum arbeitet ein Staatstheater auch mit Künstlern, die nicht vom Theater kommen? Theater ist ein Prozeß der Begegnung, langsam zwar, aber der Mut erfordert und versucht, das Fremde zu integrieren.

Kultur beschäftigt sich allgemein mit dem »Anderen«. Den »Anderen« erkennen heißt, sich selbst erkennen.

Baudrillard hat dafür eine schöne Metapher gefunden: Wir fahren auf Autobahnen – Einbahnstraßen – die alle in eine Richtung weisen: »Das Risiko des Zusammenstosses ist gering, aber die Möglichkeit der Begegnung ist gleich null. Der andere hat nur eine marginale Bedeutung«.

Die Grundform des Theaters ist jedoch der Dialog, das Nachdenken über die verschiedensten Denk- und Handlungsweisen und die Art, wie sie miteinander verbunden werden können. Zieht man eine Karte aus diesem Spiel, bricht das Haus zusammen. Vielzu oft und vielzu lange haben wir in der kulturellen Arbeit dieses unabdingbare Miteinander in seine Einzelteile zerlegt. Isolation und Unverständlichkeit, Kommunikationslosigkeit und Egozentrismus waren Folgen, die die Welt aus den Fugen brachte. Trotz oder gerade wegen der unendlichen Vielfalt an Informationsmöglichkeiten, haben wir es unterlassen, die Beziehungen zwischen den Dingen, den Menschen und ihren Lebensformen anzuerkennen. Kunst hat die Aufgabe, diese Bereiche nicht nur zu konfrontieren sondern sie auch miteinander zu verknüpfen. Denken wir an die Renaissance: da war der Künstler Handwerker, Bildhauer, Philosoph und Architekt zugleich. Heute ist er vielleicht 'nur' noch Architekt und braucht einen bildenden Künstler an seiner Seite, um »Kunst am Bau« zu garantieren.

Aufgabe einer staatlichen Kulturinstitution ist also nicht nur die Erhaltung bestehender Kultur, sondern darüber hinaus die Verantwortung, an der geistigen Tradition weiterzuarbeiten und neue Erkenntnisse zu fördern, sichtbar und erlebbar zu machen, so daß sie aktiver Bestandteil des gesamten Lebensprozesses werden.

Theater, Bildende Kunst und Film sind Bestandteile dieses Prozesses. Film ist die moderne Ausprägung der dramatischen Kunst und zugleich die Weiterentwicklung des Tafelbildes in seiner bewegten Form. Seine Kraft liegt in der Verführung zu Welten der Illusionen und Realismen, die das Theater nicht entwickeln konnte, sich aber ganz entschieden von ihnen beeinflussen ließ: in der Ästhetik, in der Ausdrucks- und Sprachweise, in der Gestik und im Aktionsduktus. Filmkunst, Theaterkunst, bildende Kunst und

technische Errungenschaften sind unweigerlich miteinander verknüpft.

Eine Beschäftigung und Auseinandersetzung mit der Verschränkung aller Künste wirkt der Desorientierung und Verlorenheit des Einzelnen entgegen, die sich seltsamerweise durch die Informationsvielfalt ergeben hat, die doch eigentlich dem besseren Kennenlernen dienen sollte. Quantität und Geschwindigkeit des Transfers aber führten zu einer Überforderung.

Peter Greenaway gehört zu den wenigen Künstlern, der durch enzyklopädisches Wissen Brücken schlägt, wo keiner mehr gewagt hat, sie zu sehen. Diesen »Brückenbauer« kann keine Institution, die kulturelle Maßstäbe setzt, außer Acht lassen, ist doch die »Brückenbauerfunktion« das beobachtende, analysierende und synthetisierende Auge des Künstlers. Das ist die Chance, Kultur als Ort des Eigenen und des Anderen zu definieren, als essentiellen Teil menschlichen Daseins.

Peter Greenaway, so haben wir ihn als Filmemacher, Maler und Ausstellungsmacher erlebt, beschäftigt sich mit Grundsatzfragen, die künstlerisches Schaffen ausmachen. Seine Kunst ist eine »Schule des Sehens«. In der Hervorhebung des Substantiellen durch oft ungewöhnliche Präsentationsformen wird der Blick des Zuschauers neu gelenkt, seine Wahrnehmung geschärft, seine Aufmerksamkeit geweckt. Er ist ein Verführer der Sinne, die Sinne zum Wesentlichen führend. So bringt er die Vielfalt unseres Denkens und Daseins zur Anschauung.

Ungewöhnliche Wege gehen, heißt ungewöhnliche Anforderungen stellen. Allen, die dieses Projekt »Projection-Frames« in München gefördert, unterstützt und mitgeholfen haben, es zu realisieren, sei hier ein großer Dank ausgesprochen. Vor allem dem Oberbürgermeister Christian Ude, der Bürgermeisterin Sabine Csampai, dem Kulturreferenten Siegfried Hummel, Andreas Rost und dem Bayerischen Kultusministerium, Eberhard Hauff, allen Referaten der Stadt, die mit Offenheit Unmögliches möglich gemacht haben.

Dank auch den privaten Sponsoren und Institutionen, ohne die diese Ausstellung im öffentlichen Raum nicht zustande gekommen wäre.

Eberhard Witt/Elisabeth Schweeger

Why should a national theatre also work with artists whose background is not the theatre? Because theatre is a testing-ground that demands the courage to confront the new and the strange, and to absorb it, if only in stages.

Culture in general has to do with the assimilation of the 'other': coming to terms with the other is to come to terms with oneself.

Baudrillard makes the same point in a neat simile: each of us travels on roads leading in one direction only – one-way streets. "The risk of collision is small, but the opportunity of meeting is almost nil. One's neighbour has very little significance."

Theatre, however, is essentially a dialogue, a reflection of widely diverse ways of thinking and behaving, and of the process of communication. Its house falls down if one of the cards is removed. Much too often and for much too long our cultural activity has been directed towards dissecting this indispensable bond into its parts. From the rifts the world has reaped only isolation and misunderstanding, failure of communication and egocentrism. Despite or even because of the infinite range of information available to us today, we have failed to recognise the connections between the material world and humanity and our way of life. It is the task of art not merely to face up to these connections but to make sense of them. In the Renaissance, for example, the artist had to be craftsman, painter, architect and philosopher all at once. Today he is perhaps still 'only' an architect and needs an artist at his side to give his form artistic intention.

The task of a national cultural institution is not only to maintain existing culture but to advance beyond it, to rework traditional ideas and to create, visualize and materialize new ones, so that they become an active, participatory force in the life-process as a whole.

Theatre, the visual arts and film are an integral part of this process. Film is both a modern form of drama and an extension of panel-painting into movement. It has the capacity to lead us into a world of illusion with a realism that the theatre cannot match, although it has been decisively influenced by the theatre in its aesthetic, its modes of expression, gesture and dialogue, its narrative and plotting. Film, theatre, art and technical achievement are inevitably linked.

An active engagement with combining and merging all the arts will prevent the disorientation and lack of focus that occasionally results from an abundance of information, though such information should properly lead to better knowledge. The speed and size of the transaction may temporarily create an overload.

Peter Greenaway is one of the few artists whose encyclopaedic knowledge builds bridges where no-one before had dared to envisage them. No institution responsible for cultural standards can ignore such 'bridge-builders', especially since 'bridging' is the artist's function – by observing, analysing and synthesizing. Hence we may enable culture as the site of definition of self and other, as an essential part of being human.

Peter Greenaway, in his career as filmmaker, painter and maker of exhibitions, has been concerned with the basic questions of the nature of art. His work is a lesson in seeing: by presenting or re-presenting things in often new, unusual ways he guides the viewer's eye, sharpens perception, alerts attention. He seduces the senses so as to lead them to the essential. He brings into frame the richness of our thinking and being.

To go down untrodden paths means to make exceptional demands. To all those who have encouraged and supported this project, and helped bring it into being, our greatest thanks. These go above all to Mayor Christian Ude, to Mayoress Sabine Csampai, to the head of cultural affairs Siegfried Hummel, to Andreas Rost, the Bayerische Kultusministerium, Eberhard Hauff, to all the municipal departments which have generously made the impossible possible. Our thanks go also to all private sponsors and institutions, without whom this exhibition in public space could never have taken place.

Eberhard Witt/Elisabeth Schweeger

ARRI is an award winner under the 'Pairing Scheme' (the National Heritage Arts Sponsorship Scheme) for its support of Peter Greenaway's THE STAIRS 2: Projection. The Scheme is managed by the Association for Business Sponsorship of the Arts (ABSA).

ARRI erhält eine Förderung durch das 'Pairing Scheme' (National Heritage Arts Sponsorship Scheme) für die Unterstützung von Peter Greenaway's THE STAIRS 2: Projektionen. Das 'Pairing Scheme' ist eine Initiative von 'The Association for Business Sponsorship of the Arts' (ABSA).

The British Council

THE STAIRS: PROJECTION – An exhibition by Peter Greenaway from 26th October to 19th November 1995 in Munich.

An event organized by the Bayerisches Staatsschauspiel/Marstall, the Kulturreferat der Landeshauptstadt München, PARTNER Unternehmensgestaltung GmbH, Stuttgart/München and Hahn Production, Munich.

Supported by the Bayerische Staatsministerium für Unterricht, Kultus, Wissenschaft und Kunst.

Sponsored by Arnold & Richter Cine Technik GmbH & Co. Betriebs KG, Deutsche Bahn AG, the British Council, Lufthansa AG, Penta Hotel München, Vitra Basel, the National Heritage Arts Sponsorship Scheme, BSW Computerrent GmbH.

The organizers wish to thank the Munich public transport system MVV and the Munich Stadtwerke for their helpfulness.

With special thanks to: Oberbürgermeister Christian Ude, Bürgermeisterin Sabine Csampai, Kulturreferent Siegfried Hummel, Dr. Andreas Rost, Bayerisches Kultusministerium, Wolfgang H. Bühler, Eberhard Hauff, Stadtwerke München, all departments of the Baureferat der Landeshauptstadt München, the Geodätisches Institut der Technischen Universität München.

Lighting Designer Reinier van Brummelen
Curator Elisabeth Schweeger
Production Assistant Simone Nickl
Production Assistant at the Marstall, Photographer Manu. Luksch
Production Manager London
Eliza Poklewski Koziell
Technical Manager, Lighting Kurt Rager
Technical Manager, Towers Dieter Hautmann
Technical Manager at the Marstall
Dieter Schmitz
Lighting at the Marstall Frank Kaster
Sound at the Marstall Peter Vogel
Assistants at the Marstall
Klaus Peinhaupt, Astrid Müller
Publicity Daniela Goldmann
Sponsor Organizers Marstall office, Kulturmanagement Häusler GmbH, Daniela Goldmann
Research Information Michel Cieutat, Dick Vaughan
German translations Thomas Bodmer, Zurich
Outline maps Stadtkartenwerk München Reproduced with the permission of the Städtischer Vermessungsamt München A7 6/95

First published in 1995 by Merrell Holberton Publishers Ltd, Axe & Bottle Court, 70 Newcomen Street, London SE1 1YT

All rights reserved
International Combined Edition:
ISBN 1 85894 022 2

Produced by Merrell Holberton Publishers
Design by Karin Dunbar Design
Typeset by SX Composing, Rayleigh
Printed in Italy by Grafiche Milani, Milan

PROJEKTION-FRAMES – Eine Ausstellung von Peter Greenaway in München vom 26. Oktober bis 19. November 1995.

Eine Veranstaltung des Bayerischen Staatsschauspiels/Marstall, des Kulturreferates der Landeshauptstadt München, der PARTNER Unternehmensgestaltung GmbH Stuttgart/München und der Hahn Produktion München.

Mit Unterstützung des Bayerischen Ministeriums für Unterricht, Kultus, Wissenschaft und Kunst.

Gesponsort von Arnold & Richter Cine Technik GmbH & Co. Betriebs KG, Deutsche Bahn AG, British Council, Lufthansa AG, Penta Hotel München, Vitra Basel, the National Heritage Arts Sponsorship Scheme, BSW Computerrent GmbH.

Die Veranstalter danken dem Münchner Verkehrs- und Tarifverbund (MVV) und den Münchner Stadtwerken für ihre kollegiale Mithilfe.

Mit besonderem Dank an: Oberbürgermeister Christian Ude, Bürgermeisterin Sabine Csampai, Kulturreferent Siegfried Hummel, Dr. Andreas Rost, Bayerisches Kultusministerium, Wolfgang H. Bühler, Eberhard Hauff, Stadtwerke München, Baureferat der Landeshauptstadt München mit allen Abteilungen, Geodätisches Institut der Technischen Universität München u.a.

Lichtdesign Reinier van Brummelen
Kurator Elisabeth Schweeger
Produktionsassistenz Simone Nickl
Produktionsassistenz Marstall, Fotografie
Manu. Luksch
Produktionsleitung London
Eliza Poklewski Koziell
Technische Leitung Licht Kurt Rager
Technische Leitung Türme Dieter Hautmann
Technische Leitung Marstall
Dieter Schmitz
Beleuchtungsmeister Marstall
Frank Kaster
Tontechnik Marstall Peter Vogel
Assistenz Marstall
Klaus Peinhaupt, Astrid Müller
Public Relations Daniela Goldmann
Sponsorakquise Marstall Büro, Kulturmanagement Häusler GmbH, Daniela Goldmann
Recherchen Michel Cieutat, Dick Vaughan
Übersetzung Thomas Bodmer, Zürich
Kartengrundlage Stadtkartenwerk München Vervielfältigt mit Genehmigung des Städtischen Vermessungsamt München A7 6/95

1995 erschienen bei Merrell Holberton Publishers Ltd, Axe & Bottle Court, 70 Newcomen Street, London SE1 1YT

Alle Rechte vorbehalten
Internationale Gesamtausgabe
ISBN 1 85894 022 2

Herstellung: Merrell Holberton Publishers
Gestaltung: Karin Dunbar Design
Satz: SX Composing, Rayleigh
Druck: Grafiche Milani, Mailand

THE STAIRS MUNICH PART ONE

THE STAIRS MÜNCHEN TEIL EINS

CONTENTS

INHALT

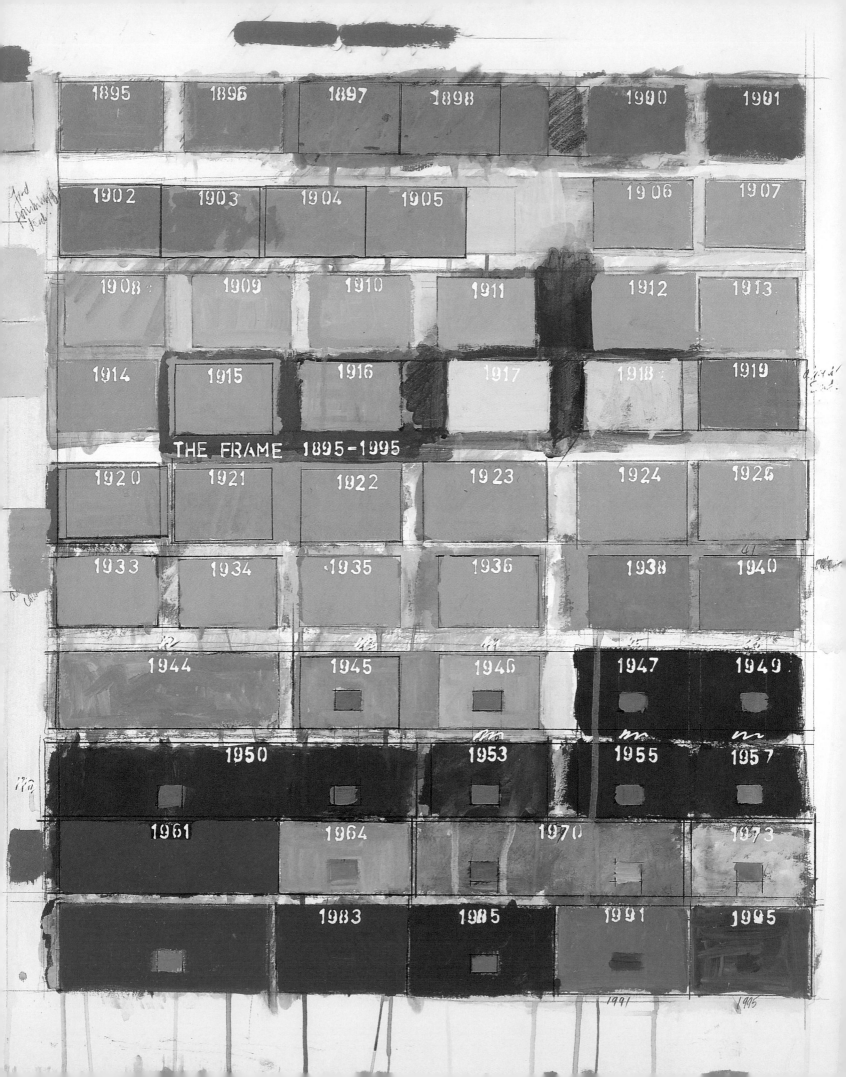

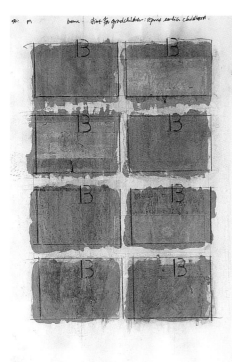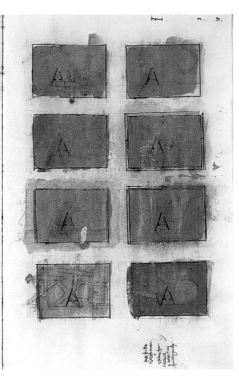

A-B Squares *from* A Framed Life *by Peter Greenaway*

A-B Quadrate. *Aus* Ein gerahmtes Leben *von Peter Greenaway*

INTRODUCTION

I am curious about the possibilities of taking cinema out of the cinema. I am curious about presenting cinema as a three-dimensional exhibition. I am curious about what constitutes a vocabulary of cinema. I am curious, I suppose, finally, in respect of the new technologies and the apparent morbidity of the old, how we are to go about re-inventing cinema.

To explore all these questions, THE STAIRS was conceived in 1992 as a series of ten investigative exhibitions to be held in ten different cities around the world. The multiplicity of disciplines that go together to make cinema are tightly interwoven, and each exhibition inevitably deals in part with them all – but it is intended that each exhibition should have one dominant theme to itself, namely:

Location	Light (Projection)
Audience	Acting
Properties	The Frame
Text	Time
Scale	Illusion

In Geneva in 1994, the subject of the THE STAIRS was Location, in Barcelona in 1997 it will be Audience. In 1998 and 1999, the subjects of Acting and Properties are to be investigated – possibly in Tokyo and Warsaw.

In Munich in 1995, the year that celebrates a hundred years of cinema, the subject is Projection.

EINLEITUNG

Mich interessiert die Frage, wie man das Kino aus dem Kino herausholen kann. Mich interessiert, das Kino in einer dreidimensionalen Ausstellung zu präsentieren. Mich interessiert, woraus das Vokabular des Kinos besteht. Und letztlich interessiert mich wohl in Anbetracht der neuen technischen Möglichkeiten und der offenbaren Gebrechlichkeit der alten, wie wir das Kino neu erfinden könnten.

Aus all diesen Gründen wurde 1992 THE STAIRS als Serie von zehn Ausstellungen untersuchenden Charakters konzipiert, die in zehn verschiedenen Städten rund um die Welt stattfinden sollen. All die verschiedenen Disziplinen, die beim Filmemachen zusammenkommen, sind eng miteinander verflochten, und so haben alle Ausstellungen zwangsläufig mit ihnen allen zu tun, doch beabsichtigt ist, daß jede Ausstellung ein Hauptthema haben soll, nämlich:

Schauplatz	Licht (Projektion)
Publikum	Schauspielern
Requisiten	Rahmen
Text	Zeit
Größenverhältnisse	Illusion

Thema der Genfer STAIRS-Ausstellung 1994 war der Schauplatz, Thema der Ausstellung in Barcelona 1997 wird das Publikum sein. 1998 und 1999 sollen die Bereiche »Requisiten« und »Schauspielern« erkundet werden, möglicherweise in Tokio und Warschau.

In München im Jahr 1995, da wir 100 Jahre Film feiern, geht es um das Thema »Projektion«.

(opposite) The Frame 1895–1995 *from* Short Frame Resumé *by Peter Greenaway*

(links) Der Rahmen 1895–1995. *Aus* Kurzes Rahmen-Resümee *von Peter Greenaway*

THE ORIGIN OF "THE STAIRS"

In 1986 I wrote an ambitious film-script called THE STAIRS which, in a narrative guise, speculatively hoped to discuss the provocations *ad nauseam* of the business of putting images with text, theatre with architecture, painting with music, selfishness with ambition. Stairs became the architectural motif and the general metaphor of the potential film (not ignoring the appropriate pun on a good hard look), relative to up-ness and down-ness, ascending and descending, flight and gravity, success and failure, Heaven and Hell … As has often been achieved with spectacular success architecturally, it was to present a platform for display, like a theatre stage raked high for excellent visibility.

Needless to say, the film-script was cumbrous and long, full of footnotes and wandering digressions. The ambitions of the subject seemed to demand a 24-hour film on three screens – a provocative impossibility ripe for oblivion. The self-reflexive nature of the project and its numerous paradoxes and contradictions seemed to suggest that cinema, to discuss itself, could be well served by some overspill activity that celebrated all its parts from the outside, indeed by some notion of the mega-cinema that is talked about but not yet realised, or certainly by some fuller event than cinema is largely at present – which is a cinema that is asked only to engage the attention of the eyes and ears of a two-hour audience obliged to sit passively in the dark staring in one direction at shadows coerced to tell a story.

The ambitious project-on-paper of THE STAIRS had been brought to conception by the manufacture of the film THE BELLY OF AN ARCHITECT, a fiction itself nudged into being by the heated mid-1980s fascination with the responsibilities of the architect. Not since Christopher Wren and the Great Fire of London, it was said, had Londoners become so impassioned about architecture.

The film's simple plot centred around the attempt of an American architect, Stourley Kracklite, to stage an exhibition in Rome, the capital city of classical architecture. It was to be a homage-exhibition to Kracklite's hero, Etienne-Louis Boullée, the almost apocryphal late eighteenth-century French architect whose reputation relies on architecture-on-paper, on buildings dedicated to abstract moral qualities, on his

DER URSPRUNG VON »THE STAIRS«

1986 schrieb ich ein ehrgeiziges Drehbuch mit dem Titel THE STAIRS. Darin sollten in erzählender Form die Provokationen erschöpfend erörtert werden, welche die Kombination von Bildern und Text, Theater und Architektur, Malerei und Musik, Egoismus und Ehrgeiz mit sich bringt. Architektonisches Motiv und übergreifende Metapher des geplanten Films waren Treppen (wobei das im Englischen aus dem Gleichklang von »stairs« = »Treppen« und »stares« = »intensive Blicke« sich ergebende Wortspiel mitberücksichtigt wurde), einerseits wegen ihrer Bezüge zu Oben und Unten, Hinauf und Hinunter, Flug und Schwerkraft, Erfolg und Scheitern, Himmel und Hölle, andererseits weil es spektakuläre architektonische Beispiele dafür gibt, wie geeignet Treppen für Präsentationen sind: Wie steil ansteigende Bühnen bieten sie eine exzellente Sicht.

Natürlich war das Drehbuch überfrachtet lang, voller Fußnoten und Abschweifungen. Das ambitiöse Thema hätte zumindest einen 24-Stunden-Film auf drei Leinwänden erfordert – eine provokative Unmöglichkeit, die reif für den Orkus war. Der selbstreflexive Aspekt des Projekts und seine zahlreichen Paradoxa und Widersprüche legten nahe, daß die Selbsterörterung des Kinos durch zusätzliche Aktivitäten unterstützt werden könnte, welche die einzelnen Bestandteile des Kinos außerhalb desselben feierten; daß eine Vorstellung geschaffen würde von dem Mega-Kino, das im Gespräch, aber nirgends verwirklicht ist, einem Erlebnis von größerer Fülle jedenfalls, als das heutige Kino in der Regel bietet, das nichts weiter leisten muß, als der Aufmerksamkeit von Augen und Ohren eines Publikums zu genügen, das zwei Stunden lang passiv im Dunkeln sitzen und immer auf denselben Fleck blicken muß, wo bewegte Schatten gezwungen sind, eine Geschichte zu erzählen.

Das auf dem Papier bestehende, ehrgeizige Projekt THE STAIRS hatte seinen Ursprung in der Arbeit am Film DER BAUCH DES ARCHITEKTEN, einer erfundenen Geschichte, die aus den hitzigen Diskussionen Mitte der achtziger Jahre über die Verantwortung des Architekten hervorging. Es hieß, seit den Zeiten von Christopher Wren (1632–1723), der nach dem großen Brand von London (1666) zum General-Architekten des Wiederaufbaus ernannt worden war, hätten die Londoner sich nie mehr so über Architektur ereifert.

Die simple Handlung des Films drehte sich um den Versuch eines amerikanischen Architekten, Stourley Kracklite, in Rom, der Hauptstadt der klassischen Architektur, eine Ausstellung zu veranstalten. Sie sollte eine Hommage an Kracklites Idol sein, den beinahe apokryphen französischen Architekten

The Etienne-Louis Boullée Exhibition at the Victor Emmanuel Building in Rome from The Belly of an Architect

Die Étienne-Louis-Boullée-Ausstellung im Vittorio-Emmanuele-Denkmal in Rom. Aus Der Bauch des Architekten

The Grandiose Designs of Etienne Louis-Boullée from The Belly of an Architect

Die grandiosen Entwürfe Étienne-Louis Boullées. Aus Der Bauch des Architekten

(opposite) Staircase of the Laurenziana Library, Florence, designed by Michelangelo

(links) Michelangelos Treppenhaus der Bibliotheca Laurenziana, Florenz

11

Stourley Kracklite descends the steps of the Victor Emmanuel Monument, from The Belly of an Architect

Stourley Kracklite schreitet die Stufen des Vittorio-Emmanuele-Denkmals hinab. Aus Der Bauch des Architekten

The Etienne-Louis Boullée Exhibition at the Victor Emanuel Building in Rome from The Belly of an Architect

Die Étienne-Louis-Boullée-Ausstellung. Aus Der Bauch des Architekten

ability to inspire both Robespierre and Albert Speer, on monuments of impossible scale, and on a curious celebration of gloomy immortality.

The exhibition was mounted in the extravagant Victor-Emmanuel Monument in the Piazza Venezia in Rome. It contained all the orthodox exhibits – plans, prints, models, maps, drawings, correspondence, even the occasional fragment of masonry, but overwhelmingly it was dominated by the numerous statements of intent and ambition made by Boullée on behalf of Architecture. The notion of the evidence of architectural dreams (and perhaps nightmares) self-consciously exhibited in Rome, in close proximity to the architecture that inspired them – the idea of buildings being seen in the abstract and from a sideways glance – was attractive.

It seemed to me that Kracklite's attempt to celebrate the man and the medium he revered, but by whom and by which he was so ambiguously and frustratingly thwarted, might be an appropriate base for a consideration of cinema.

The film-script of THE STAIRS became a proposition – retaining the same title as the projected film along with its architectural and metaphorical implications – for a series of exhibitions on the nature of cinema.

des späten 18. Jahrhunderts, Étienne-Louis Boullée, der seinen Ruhm größtenteils nur auf dem Papier bestehenden Konzepten von Gebäuden verdankte, die abstrakten moralischen Eigenschaften gewidmet waren; der dem Vernehmen nach Robespierre wie Albert Speer inspiriert hatte; der Denkmäler von nicht zu verwirklichender Größe entwarf und dessen Werk eine sonderbar düstere Feier der Unsterblichkeit darstellte.

Die Ausstellung wurde im extravaganten Vittorio-Emmanuele-Monument an der Piazza Venezia in Rom eingerichtet. Sie umfaßte die üblichen Ausstellungsstücke – Baupläne, Drucke, Modelle, Stadtpläne, Zeichnungen, Briefe und Fragmente von Mauerwerk –, doch vor allem eine überwältigende Zahl von ehrgeizigen Absichtserklärungen Boullées zum Thema Architektur. Die Idee, diese Zeugen architektonischer (Alb-)Träume jenen römischen Bauten gegenüberzustellen, von denen sie angeregt waren, und Gebäude damit gleichzeitig als Abstrakta und aus ungewöhnlichen Blickwinkeln zu zeigen, war attraktiv.

Mir schien, Kracklites Versuch, den Mann und das Medium zu feiern, die er verehrte und an deren Zwiespältigkeit er scheiterte, wäre auch für eine Erörterung des Kinos geeignet.

Das Drehbuch THE STAIRS entwickelte sich also – unter Beibehaltung des Titels und der architektonischen und metaphorischen Bezüge – zum Konzept für eine Reihe von Ausstellungen über das Wesen des Kinos.

THE CINEMA

The cinema, they say, is the medium for all seasons. Perhaps it is not a single medium at all, but a plethora of possible ways to communicate hoping for synthesis. It is writing illustrated, theatre recorded, the talking novel, painting on the move, image serviced to music. Just now that cinema celebrates its first centenary and is a medium ripe for the re-invention of itself, there is evidence to believe that all art moves towards the condition of film. Painters, writers, playwrights, composers, choreographers – creators indeed who we could say should know better – have eager aspirations to make films, and if not to make them, then to debate endlessly the possibilities of making them. Is this condition to which art moves that of the ultimate mixed-media? – which could be a way of saying that cinema is still a mongrel hoping for pedigree status, still a hybrid awaiting official recognition? Still a safe-deposit box where you can stash away any currency whatsoever? The issue goes beyond cinema's reputation for excess in publicity, gossip, scandal, money, fame, infamy, expense and hubris, and is bound tightly to the notion that cinema is considered to be the true medium of the twentieth century, possible thesaurus of all dreams and all ambitions. Yet is it really so all-embracing, does it really have the ability to inflame the imagination profitably as its apologists believe?

Perhaps a cinema history of one hundred years is both long enough to say that cinema has arrived to stay, and short enough to argue that what we have seen so far has probably been a sort of cinema prologue. Cinema is still mimicking theatre – the medium essentially (certainly in the West) of the enacted word. It is still in the business of transferring text into film. What is it about cinema that it disturbs our confidence in its primacy as a medium? Most importantly perhaps: have there really been films of which it can be said, their content could not be presented in any other way as effectively? Indeed have we seen a film yet?

Eisenstein is reported having said to Disney that only he, Disney, truly made films. Disney's whole cinematic world was truly invented, with no reliance on the limiting photographic representation that constantly impoverishes cinema by showing us what reality is like. Against this implication, can film ever truly be non-mimetic if it relies on

DAS KINO

Das Kino, sagt man, sei ein Allzweck-Medium. Vielleicht ist es aber gar kein einzelnes Medium, sondern eine Vielzahl möglicher Kommunikationsarten, die auf eine Synthese hoffen. Es ist illustriertes Schreiben, aufgezeichnetes Theater, ein sprechender Roman, Malerei in Bewegung, Bilder im Dienste der Musik. Während das Kino sein hundertjähriges Bestehen feiert und reif dafür ist, sich neu zu erfinden, deutet einiges darauf hin, daß alle Künste sich auf den Film zubewegen. Maler, Schriftsteller, Dramatiker, Komponisten, Choreographen – schöpferische Menschen, von denen man meinen sollte, daß sie es besser wüßten – sind ganz begierig darauf, Filme zu drehen oder – wenn sie keine drehen – die Möglichkeit davon endlos zu erörtern. Bedeutet dies, daß das Kino als Inbegriff des Multimedialen aufgefaßt wird, oder anders gesagt, daß das Kino noch immer eine Straßenmischung ist, die sich nach einem Stammbaum sehnt, noch immer eine Kreuzung, die auf offizielle Anerkennung hofft? Ist das Kino eine Art Safe, in dem alle möglichen Währungen verstaut werden können? Das Kino gilt als exzessiv, was Werbung, Gerüchte, Skandale, Gagen, Berühmtheit, Verrufenheit, Kosten und Selbstüberschätzung betrifft, doch darüber hinaus gilt es auch als das eigentliche Medium des 20. Jahrhunderts, als möglicher Thesaurus aller Träume und Ambitionen. Doch ist das Kino wirklich so allumfassend, hat es wirklich die Fähigkeit, die Phantasie auf so lohnende Weise anzuregen, wie seine Verfechter behaupten?

Vielleicht ist seine hundertjährige Geschichte lang genug für die Feststellung, das Kino werde sich halten, und kurz genug für die Behauptung, was wir bisher gesehen hätten, sei erst eine Art Vorspiel gewesen. Noch immer imitiert das Kino das Theater, welches zumindest im Westen das Medium des dargestellten Wortes ist. Noch immer ist es damit beschäftigt, Text in Film umzusetzen. Woran liegt es, daß wir die Überlegenheit des Kinos als Medium anzweifeln? Und die wichtigste Frage: Gibt es Filme, von denen sich tatsächlich sagen läßt, ihr Inhalt hätte sich auf keine andere Weise ebenso wirkungsvoll vermitteln lassen? Haben wir je einen eigentlichen Film gesehen?

Eisenstein soll Disney gesagt haben, er, Disney, sei der einzige, der wirklich Filme mache. Disneys Kinowelt war von Grund auf erfunden, ohne Rücksicht auf die Beschränkungen einer fotografische Abbildung der Wirklichkeit; denn schließlich wird das Kino dadurch ärmer, daß uns immer wieder in Erinnerung gerufen wird, wie die Wirklichkeit aussieht. Kann das Kino denn je etwas anderes als mimetisch sein, solange es von fotografischen Abbildungen ausgeht? Wäre

Frame from The Draughtsman's Contract

Aus Der Kontrakt des Zeichners

photographic representation? If only Eisenstein had been Disney, cinema could have made a truly profitable push into enlightenment. As it is – alas – we could say the opposite has happened.

This year, 1995, sees a hundred years of sprocketed celluloid strips passing across a beam of white light – a technology that has spawned an aesthetic (perhaps this is always a definition of an art-form). In Europe, one hundred years is apparently long enough for a new technology-aesthetic to complete its cycle from birth to at least senescence. Italian fresco painting, North European linseed-oil painting, nineteenth-century opera, the symphony ... all were furiously busy for about a hundred years before the form became fixed and fossilized, a curiosity kept alive by nostalgia, or special privilege, or academia. Perhaps there is a correlation between such a cycle and the length of one super-generation, the three-part generation of a living memory – father, son and grandson. Few have informed memories of great grandparents or great grandchildren and beyond living memory the aesthetic-technology loses its clout; something new is required. Perhaps there is evidence that cinema is about to respect this pattern.

However, with cinema something new indeed had happened that had never happened before. Cinema developed characteristics that could easily be recognized through a very large body of work manufactured all over the world, touching every culture; and any culture which has not manufactured cinema can, with little effort, become its spectator. This rapid and invasive spread of a medium of communication is unique; it has never happened so thoroughly and so swiftly before. In fact it probably did not need one hundred years: possibly fifty years would have been enough – 1895 to 1945, from the end of the nineteenth century to the end of the Second World War.

Perhaps this universality has been cinema's problem, for in most places where it has travelled and been successful, it has largely remained an imported act of communication, with the local culture taking it on wholesale without making, or being able to make, a significant contribution. Because of the colonizing strengths of its prime manufacturers, it has been difficult indeed to change it by adoption or adaptation. European and American cinema are very much alike. All

Eisenstein doch Disney gewesen, dann hätte das Kino einen wirklich lohnenden Vorstoß Richtung Aufklärung gemacht. Doch leider müssen wir sagen, daß das Gegenteil geschehen ist.

In diesem Jahr, 1995, sind es hundert Jahre her, seit die ersten perforierten Zelluloid-streifen einen weißen Lichtstrahl durchquert haben und ein bestimmtes technisches Mittel eine eigene Ästhetik geschaffen hat – vielleicht ist dies die Definition jeder Kunstform. In Europa scheinen hundert Jahre lang genug zu sein, damit eine neue technisch bedingte Ästhetik den Zyklus von der Geburt bis zur – sagen wir mal – Vergreisung durchläuft. Italienische Freskenmalerei, nordeuropäische Leinöl-Malerei, die Opernform des 19. Jahrhunderts, die Symphonie – rund ein Jahrhundert lang war da jeweils rasend viel los, dann erstarrte die Form, wurde zu einem Fossil, einer Kuriosität, die einzig noch aus Nostalgie, dank besonderen Privilegien oder aus akademischem Interesse am Leben erhalten wurde. Vielleicht besteht ein Zusammenhang zwischen einem solchen Zyklus und der Länge der Generationenfolge Vater-Sohn-Enkel, welche von der Erinnerung noch bewältigt werden kann. Die wenigsten Leute haben präzise Erinnerungen an Urgroßeltern oder Großenkel, und außerhalb dieses von der Erinnerung zu bewältigenden Zeitraums überlebt sich auch eine technisch bedingte Ästhetik, wird es Zeit für etwas Neues. Vielleicht ließen sich Anzeichen dafür finden, daß auch das Kino diesem Schema folgt.

Doch ist mit dem Kino etwas Neues geschehen, das noch nie geschehen war: Das Kino entwickelte innerhalb einer in aller Welt entstehenden Masse an Werken Eigenschaften, die überall leicht erkennbar waren, jede Kultur berührten; und selbst in Kulturen, wo keine Filme gedreht wurden, konnte man ohne großen Aufwand Filmzuschauer werden. Diese rasend schnelle flächendeckende Verbreitung eines Kommunikationsmediums ist einzigartig; so rasch und gründlich war dies noch nie geschehen. Ja es brauchte auch keine hundert Jahre dazu, die Zeit von 1895 bis 1945, vom Ende des 19. Jahrhunderts bis zum Ende des zweiten Weltkriegs, dürfte gereicht haben.

Vielleicht ist gerade diese Universalität das Problem des Kinos, denn an den meisten Orten, wohin es kam und wo es Erfolg hatte, blieb es ein importierter Kommunikations-vorgang, der von der lokalen Kultur geschluckt wurde, ohne daß diese einen eigenen Beitrag von Belang geleistet hätte oder hätte leisten können. Weil die Haupt-Verbreiter des Kinos große Kolonisatoren waren, war es schwierig, das Medium durch Adoption oder Adaption zu verändern. Das europäische und das amerikanische Kino sind sich sehr ähnlich. Englischsprachige Filme

English-speaking cinema is virtually indistinguishable. Contemporary Chinese and Japanese cinema is not unlike the films of America and Europe in structure and narrative. All cinematic cultures now relate to the American cinema, the dominance of which is supreme. To stay vigorously alive a medium must keep re-inventing itself, and if all cultures contribute the same characteristics, perhaps that has now become improbable.

Cinema has always been a complex technological medium; it has nearly always required considerable collaborative effort across many disciplines, and from its very earliest creation it has been a large financial enterprise – three reasons perhaps which have inhibited continued serious exploration and innovation. If we make comparisons of the advances in language, structure and territory that have been colonized by painting and literature in those same hundred years, then the cinema has been very conservative. Its technological characteristics – though complex compared to the manipulation of the pen or the brush – have basically changed little since its double inception, the manufacture of a moving picture around 1895 and its linkage with synchronized sound around 1927. As far as narrative development, structure and dramatic vocabulary are concerned, a film-maker like the much respected Scorsese, for example, still makes the same films as D.W. Griffith.

Whether because it is inherent in the medium, or because it has become a condition of cinema's marketing ... has cinema's realisation of its full potential as the trumpeted seventh art been strangely curtailed?

Whether we believe this is true or not, I am certain many would have criticisms to make. In general and in particular, the ten exhibitions of THE STAIRS argue these criticisms and celebrate its potential in the face of cinema's imminent re-invention. Though the issues could be variously itemized, some which concern my interest are briefly introduced here under four headings: Location, Narrative, Audience, Materiality.

lassen sich kaum nach Nationalitäten unterscheiden. Zeitgenössische chinesische und japanische Filme sind in Struktur und Erzählweise nicht grundsätzlich anders als amerikanische und europäische, und die Filmkulturen aller Länder sind heute der amerikanischen verwandt, die das filmkulturelle Geschehen absolut dominiert. Um bei Kräften zu bleiben, muß sich ein Medium andauernd neu erfinden, doch wenn alle Kulturen ein und dasselbe beitragen, ist das jetzt vielleicht nicht mehr möglich.

Das Kino ist immer ein technisch komplexes Medium gewesen, es hat fast immer großer gemeinsamer Anstrengungen von Vertretern der verschiedensten Disziplinen bedurft, und von Anfang an ist es immer eine größere finanzielle Unternehmung gewesen; dies mögen drei Gründe dafür sein, weshalb der Forschergeist und die Erneuerungslust gebremst wurden. Wenn wir uns zum Vergleich die sprachlichen, strukturellen und territorialen Fortschritte, die es während derselben hundert Jahre in der Malerei und der Literatur gegeben hat, ansehen, erweist sich das Kino als äußerst konservativ. An seinen technischen Gegebenheiten – die im Vergleich zum Führen einer Feder oder eines Pinsels zwar komplex sind – hat sich seit den beiden grundlegenden Erfindungen – der Herstellung eines bewegten Bildes um 1895 und dessen Verbindung mit synchron aufgezeichnetem Ton um 1927 – kaum etwas verändert. Und was erzählerische Entwicklung, Struktur und dramatisches Vokabular betrifft, dreht ein so hoch geschätzter Filmemacher wie Martin Scorsese immer noch die gleichen Filme wie D.W. Griffith.

Liegt es denn nun am Medium selbst oder an seiner Vermarktung, daß das mit großem Trara als siebte Kunst gefeierte Kino in der Realisation all seiner Möglichkeiten so sonderbar beschnitten worden ist?

Wie auch immer, ich bin jedenfalls überzeugt, daß es einiges zu kritisieren gibt. Die zehn Ausstellungen im Rahmen von THE STAIRS formulieren diese Kritik und feiern das Potential des Kinos angesichts seiner unmittelbar bevorstehenden Neuerfindung. Es ließen sich verschiedene Diskussionsthemen aufzählen; einige, die mich besonders interessieren, kommen auf den folgenden Seiten unter den Überschriften »Der Schauplatz«, »Die Erzählweise«, »Das Publikum«, »Die Stofflichkeit« zur Sprache.

LOCATION

I am sure that every constructed drama needs a sense of location, whether it is fact or fiction, real or imaginary, or – and this is the most usual state of affairs – a composite re-creation of a fictional place in a factual environment.

I have always been fascinated by a special sense of *genius loci*, which is a amalgam not just of geographical placing in architecture or landscape, but of a sense of timing – of day or of history, of continuity in a drama, of the presence of a group of characters in a set environment lending their noise and warmth to animate it. Whereas certainly a painting, a stage-set or a photograph can be memorably rich with the possibility of evoking location, the successful re-enactment of place is often a film's most memorable but intangible excitement, creating impossible demands in the spectator's imagination for a re-visit for further contemplation – a literal desire or 'wish to be there'. Antonioni is a master at creating such ambience.

For a film-maker to fabricate this sense of location is not easy – there are no rules, no list of objects, no table of angles or agenda of lighting that can be consulted. If this indeed is something unique to cinema, I have often wondered how it would be possible to prolong, emphasize and develop this desirable state of interest, to provide opportunity for re-visit and re-contemplation, and to experience the sense of location under different circumstances – which might well mean in different weathers, in different lights, with different company, in different silences. From the position of a film-maker, in selecting a time and deciding on an edit once these characteristics are placed on film, when is the right time and what is the correct angle, and which is the most effective light to experience the specifics of a sense of location?

The practice of creating multiple captured 'takes' of an action or event is unique to cinema. Each take records almost inevitable small differences, but film usage deems it practicable – usually in the pursuit of narrative – that only one take should be used. Can you be certain of selecting and using the best take – especially if it is not the credibility of an acting performance that is governing the decision? I have repeatedly been excited and perplexed by the decision-making process when the changing light is the main criterion

DER SCHAUPLATZ

Ich bin überzeugt, daß jedes konstruierte Drama der Situierung an einem bestimmten Ort bedarf, einem tatsächlichen oder fiktiven, realen oder erfundenen; tatsächlich wird in der Regel meist aus verschiedenen Elementen in einer realen Umgebung ein fiktiver Ort geschaffen.

Die besondere Atmosphäre eines Ortes, sein Genius loci, hat mich schon immer fasziniert. Darunter verstehe ich ein Amalgam aus geographischer Plazierung in einem architektonischen Kontext oder einer Landschaft, aber auch aus der Stimmung eines Zeitpunkts (Tageszeit, historischer Zeitpunkt), des dramatischen Ablaufs, der Anwesenheit einer Gruppe von Figuren in einer bestimmten Umgebung, die sie durch ihre Präsenz mit Geräuschen und Wärme beleben. Nun können ein Gemälde, ein Bühnenbild oder ein Foto bemerkenswert viel von einem bestimmten Ort vermitteln, doch ist das Evozieren, das erfolgreiche Heraufbeschwören eines bestimmten Ortes oft das, was uns von einem Film am stärksten in Erinnerung bleibt, so wenig greifbar dieses Gefühl auch sein mag, das in der Phantasie der Zuschauer den unmöglichen Wunsch weckt, an den Ort zurückzukehren, um ihn eingehender betrachten zu können, den eigentlichen Wunsch, dabeizusein. Antonioni ist ein Meister im Schaffen dieser Stimmungen.

Es ist nicht einfach für einen Filmemacher, dieses Gefühl eines Ortes herzustellen: Es gibt keine Regeln, keine Liste von Gegenständen, keine Aufstellung von Blickwinkelen und Lichtquellen, die sich nachschlagen ließe. Wenn wir es hier tatsächlich mit einer einzigartigen Eigenschaft des Kinos zu tun haben, habe ich mich oft gefragt, wie sich dieses wünschenswerte Interesse verlängern, verstärken und entwickeln ließe, wie man die Gelegenheit schaffen könnte, zu einem Schauplatz zurückzukehren und ihn eingehender zu betrachten, ihn unter verschiedenen Umständen zu erleben, also unterschiedlichen Wetter- und Lichtverhältnissen, in wechselnder Gesellschaft, in verschiedenen Arten der Stille. Für einen Filmemacher, der einen Zeitpunkt auswählen muß, zu dem diese Eigenschaften auf Film festgehalten werden, stellen sich die Fragen: Wann ist der richtige Zeitpunkt, welches der korrekte Blickwinkel, welches das Licht, das die spezifischen Eigenschaften eines bestimmten Schauplatzes am besten zur Geltung bringt?

Die filmische Praxis, daß von einer Handlung oder einem Ereignis verschiedene »Takes« aufgenommen werden, ist einzigartig. Jeder Take unterscheidet sich von den anderen zwangsläufig durch kleine Unterschiede, doch es ist im Film – meist aus erzählerischen Gründen – üblich, nur einen Take zu

for the manufacture of a cinematic image, and have frequently wanted to use all the takes that might record the same action ten times as an afternoon moves into evening, as an evening moves into night – each with its particular atmospheric difference which can only be enhanced by comparison with its neighbours.

The suggestion that the film experience should be abandoned in favour of a visit to the 'real' place under consideration does not provide an answer to these various location problems. It is more than likely that the 'real' places do not exist, or, if they do superficially exist in relationship to some visitable map-location, then the circumstances of their existence on film are not likely to be perpetrated 'in reality'.

The ambitions indicated by these questions suggest several objectives. They certainly ask for much longer films where 'place' has a high demand on our attention. Perhaps they demand films without end, indeed endless films. They ask for an active and not a passive interaction between film and spectator, and they demand an almost Cubist approach towards multiple viewing, one that might include location specifics, maps, plans, and a hold on the location's time and history.

Each exhibition of THE STAIRS, whatever its particular theme, seeks to prize and reproduce the possibilities of the re-visitable *genius loci*, which is why the exhibitions are organized in 'real' spaces with public accessibility, bringing with them the patina of use and acknowledgement of time. Any sense of exclusivity is limited to the experience itself, not organized around private or special time-limited access, and certainly without any conditioning of the kind normally associated with a conventional cinema projection space.

verwenden. Wie will man sicher sein, daß man den besten Take auswählt und verwendet – besonders wenn nicht die Glaubwürdigkeit einer schauspielerischen Leistung das Kriterium für die Entscheidung ist? Der Entscheidungsprozeß, bei dem Veränderungen des Lichts das Hauptkriterium für die Herstellung eines Filmbildes waren, hat mich wiederholt begeistert und verwirrt: Oft hätte ich am liebsten alle Takes verwendet, welche zehnmal die gleiche Handlung festhielten, während der Nachmittag dem Abend wich, der Abend der Nacht – jeder Take mit seiner eigenen atmosphärischen Besonderheit, die durch den Vergleich mit seinen Nachbarn erst deutlich gemacht wurde.

Der Vorschlag, angesichts solcher Schauplatz-Probleme doch die Ebene des Films zu verlassen und lieber den betreffenden »realen« Ort aufzusuchen, ist keine Lösung. Die Wahrscheinlichkeit ist zehn zu eins, daß es diese »realen« Orte gar nicht gibt, und falls sie im weitesten Sinn doch mit einem besuchbaren Ort auf einer Landkarte zu tun haben, wird sich ihre Existenz im Film kaum in die Realität umsetzen lassen.

Aus all diese Fragen ergeben sich verschiedene Konsequenzen. Zum einen der Wunsch nach viel längeren Filmen, worin den Schauplätzen ein Großteil unserer Aufmerksamkeit zukommt. Vielleicht auch nach Filmen, die kein Ende haben. Außerdem nicht nach passiver Konsumation, sondern aktiver Auseinandersetzung des Publikums mit einem Film, nach einem fast schon kubistischen Zugang im Sinne einer vielfältigen Art der Betrachtung, unter Berücksichtigung der Eigenheiten eines Schauplatzes, von Plänen, Grundrissen, der Geschichte und der Tageszeit.

Jede einzelne Ausstellung im Rahmen von THE STAIRS – egal welches ihr eigenes Thema ist – hat zum Ziel, den Genius loci begehbarer Schauplätze hervorzuheben und wiederzugeben. Aus diesem Grund finden die Ausstellungen an »realen«, der Öffentlichkeit zugänglichen Orten statt, welche die Patina des Gebrauchs und der verflossenen Zeit aufweisen. Exklusiv ist nur die Erfahrung der einzelnen Betrachterinnen und Betrachter; die Ausstellungen sind nicht nur bestimmten Leuten oder nur eine bestimmte Zeit lang zugänglich, und vor allem haben sie nichts im Sinn mit all jenen Zwängen, welchen man normalerweise in einem konventionellen Film-Projektionsraum ausgesetzt ist.

Frame from The Draughtsman's Contract

Aus Der Kontrakt des Zeichners

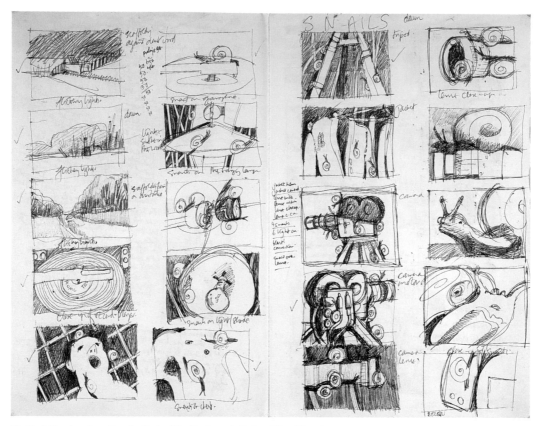

The Snail Storyboard marking the finale of the film from A Zed and Two Noughts
Das Schnecken-Storyboard zum schluß von Ein Z & zwei Nullen

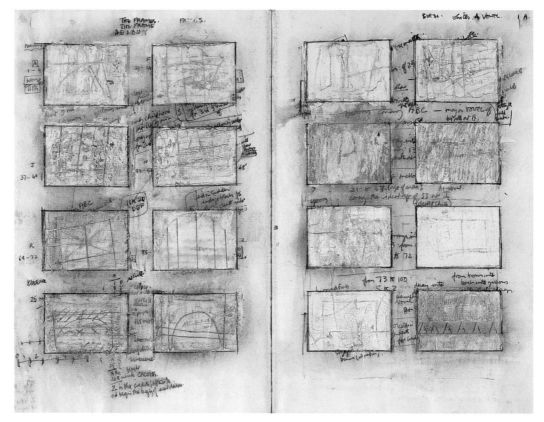

Pink Graffiti *from* A Framed Life *by Peter Greenaway*
Rosa Graffiti. *Aus* Ein gerahmtes Leben *von Peter Greenaway*

THE FRAME

From a painter's point of view at least, the film-maker and his audience should both perhaps be irritated first by the rigour of cinema's insistence on the rectangular frame, and secondly by that frame's fixed aspect-ratio – the relationship of the vertical to the horizontal axis.

Contemporary film-directors have at best three aspect-ratios to choose from – though the demands of television and its hold over the finances and therefore aesthetics of cinema threaten to reduce this to only one, the ratio of 1 to 1.33 of the proscribed box-frame of the domestic television monitor.

The example of Renaissance painting gave the frame to the stage, so that our perception of ballet, opera and theatre is almost exclusively of a performance inside and under a rectangular proscenium arch; it gave the notion of a rectangular frame to the photograph, to cinema and to television in a historical sequence that continued to perpetuate four right-angles and four straight sides. Despite numerous Baroque and Rococo practitioners investigating non-regular shapes, the size and proportions of the painting frame in the last four hundred years have generally remained conservative, centreing around the 1 to 1.66 ratio used in the wide cinema screen, though this particular mean is often up-ended to make the vertical proportion longer, to suit the needs of portrait-painters executing full-length portraits. This proportion may, no doubt, be related to the golden section, a harmonious proportion arrived at by those with no special training in mathematics and no special knowledge or good taste or 'eye'.

However, perhaps the ever decreasing choice imposed by commercial and industrial standards has tightened the frame-ratio to such a point that it must – in the same way as other tightening strictures have operated in other fields – explode. Painting, as always, has set the pace. The idea of the heavily framed painted image has found less and less favour over the last hundred years, and the last three decades have seen it largely evaporate.

The photograph is still dominated in practice by the demands of its life-blood reproduction in books, magazines and newspapers, which are all obsessed with the rectilinear page – though the aspect-ratios of a photo-

DER RAHMEN

Schon allein im Vergleich mit der Malerei sollten sich Filmemacher und ihr Publikum daran stoßen, daß im Kino einerseits stur an einem rechtwinkligen Rahmen festgehalten wird und dessen Verhältnis von der Höhe zur Breite – das Bildformat – normiert und fixiert ist.

Die Filmemacher unserer Zeit haben bestenfalls drei Bildformate zur Auswahl, und die Erfordernisse des Fernsehens – welches über die Finanzierung und damit auch die Ästhetik des Kinos entscheidet – drohen diese auf ein einziges Format zu reduzieren, womit das Kistenformat des häuslichen Fernsehbildschirms von 1 : 1,33 als einziges übrigbliebe.

Dem Vorbild der Renaissance-Malerei entsprechend erhielten in der Folge auch Bühnen einen Rahmen, weshalb wir heute Ballett, Oper und Theater fast ausschließlich innerhalb eines rechtwinkligen Bühnenrahmens zu sehen bekommen. So kam das Foto zu einem rechtwinkligen Rahmen, das Kino und das Fernsehen, und die ganze Zeit hindurch wurden die vier rechten Winkel und die vier geraden Linien aufrechterhalten. Zahlreichen Barock- und Rokoko-Malern zum Trotz, die unregelmäßige Formen ausprobierten, läßt sich beim Vergleich mit den eingeschränkten Kinoleinwand-Formaten keine besondere Freiheit der Maler in der Auswahl ihrer Rahmen feststellen. Betrachten wir uns die Rahmen von Gemälden der letzten 400 Jahre, so überwiegen, was Größe und Proportion betrifft, konservative Normen im Bereich des 1 : 1,66 Formats des Breitwand-Kinos, wobei dieses Verhältnis oft umgedreht wird, damit die längere Vertikale von Porträtmalern für Ganzporträts genutzt werden kann. Diese Proportion hat bestimmt etwas mit der Idee des Goldenen Schnitts zu tun, einer harmonischen Proportion, die Leuten entspricht, die keine besondere Ausbildung in Mathematik, kein Fachwissen, aber auch weder Geschmack noch ein gutes Auge haben.

Doch vielleicht hat sich unter dem Druck der kommerziellen und industriellen Normen die Auswahl an Formaten mittlerweile dermaßen reduziert, daß – wie auch schon geschehen – die Unerträglichkeit der Einschränkungen eine Explosion zur Folge hat. Einmal mehr dürfte die Malerei als Schrittmacher wirken. Die Idee eines schweren Rahmens um ein Gemälde hat im Lauf der letzten hundert Jahre andauernd an Attraktivität verloren, und im Lauf der letzten drei Jahrzehnte ist er fast ganz verschwunden.

Die Fotografie wird in der Praxis immer noch dominiert von den Zwängen ihrer lebenswichtigen Reproduktion in Büchern, Zeitschriften und Zeitungen, die alle von der Rechtwinkligkeit der Seiten besessen sind.

A Frame around the Masque Dancers, from Prospero's Books

Rahmen um die Tänzerinnen beim Maskenspiel. Aus Prosperos Bücher
(Marc Guillaumot)

A Frame around the Crew of the Drowned Ship, from Prospero's Books

Rahmen um die Besatzung des untergegangenen Schiffes. Aus Prosperos Bücher
(Marc Guillaumot)

A Baroque Frame around the Anatomy Lesson, from
Prospero's Books

Barocker Rahmen um die Anatomie-Lektion. Aus
Prosperos Bücher
(Marc Guillaumot)

graph are often very sensibly related to its content in a way missing from the other visual media, if only because cropped at the instigation of the print-editor rather than the photographer.

Industrial and commercial standards have placed an iron hand on the standard TV frame. The potential of the High Definition Televison Experiment with its hopeful 1 to 1.77 ratio was doomed not least because every TV set in the world would have had to be changed – a bonanza for those who controlled the new invention, a prohibitive restriction for those who did not. The explosion of the frame in television may well come through the demands of Virtual Reality which operates in a representation of space that equates with our own vision of it, and therefore does not need a frame. In cinema, the large-screen formats Imax and Omnimax have the viewer sitting very close to the screen, and have frame-edges that are so large they are generally beyond the human visual periphery, hence eliminating the frame.

The frame is artificial, a construct and a device. It does not exist in nature. Has it really established itself as an unalterable necessity? And if it has to stay, does it have to be so rigid and inflexible?

The exhibitions of THE STAIRS continually wish to question the dogma of the frame, if only, in the first instance, to demonstrate its persistence, which is so rarely questioned. But the questioning should continue, to ask about the flat, two-dimensional aspect of the cinematic illusion and to see, among other propositions, if perhaps its demise or transformation can be encouraged, at least initially, by investigation whether the frame can be changed at will to complement its content. To cite extremes, this could imply, for example, a long thin vertical frame for a giraffe's neck, and a long low horizontal frame for a snake travelling across the grass. This approach has long been a preserve of the comic-book strip, whose enviably sophisticated re-arrangement of flat picture-space has, curiously, been ignored by all those current cinematic attempts to put comic-book characters on to celluloid – retreading them yet again into the tedious linear narrative of the inflexible cinema rectangle.

Allerdings werden die Proportionen der Fotos oft auf eine so vernünftige Weise ihrem Inhalt angepaßt, wie dies in den anderen visuellen Medien nicht geschieht, wobei der Ausschnitt freilich meist von einem Bildredakteur und nicht vom Fotografen bestimmt wird.

Industrielle und kommerzielle Standards haben das Fernsehbild eisern im Griff. Das Experiment High Definition Television, dessen Proportion von 1 : 1,77 allerlei Hoffnungen geweckt hatte, scheiterte nicht zuletzt daran, daß jedes Fernsehgerät der Welt geändert hätte werden müssen, was eine Goldgrube für diejenigen gewesen wäre, welche über die neue Erfindung verfügten, und für alle anderen eine nicht tolerierbare Einschränkung. Mag sein, daß die Zerstörung des Rahmens im Fernsehen mit Virtual Reality erfolgen wird, welches von einer Wahrnehmung des Raums ausgeht, die unserer eigenen Sicht entspricht und deshalb keinen Rahmen braucht. Die Begrenzungen der übergroßen Kinoleinwand-Formate Imax und Omnimax, bei denen der Betrachter ganz dicht vor der Leinwand sitzt, liegen in der Regel außerhalb des menschlichen Gesichtsfelds, womit das Gefühl eines Rahmens entfällt.

Das Rahmen genannte Gebilde ist etwas Künstliches, ein Konstrukt. Einen Rahmen gibt es nicht in der Natur. Hat er sich denn mittlerweile wirklich als unumgängliche Notwendigkeit durchgesetzt? Und wenn er denn erhalten bleibt, muß er dann so starr und unflexibel sein?

Die Ausstellungen unter dem Motto THE STAIRS möchten das Dogma des Rahmens immer wieder in Frage stellen. Das beginnt damit, daß auf sein Vorhandensein aufmerksam gemacht wird, das für das Publikum in der Regel gar kein Thema ist. Doch darüber hinaus sollten wir uns fragen, warum wir an der platten Zweidimensionalität der filmischen Illusion festhalten und ob erste Schritte zu deren Abschaffung oder Umwandlung damit unternommen werden könnten, daß wir ausprobieren, ob sich der Rahmen nicht nach Wunsch dem jeweiligen Inhalt anpassen ließe. Im Extremfall liefe dies auf einen schmalen hochformatigen Rahmen für den Hals einer Giraffe hinaus und auf ein niedriges Breitformat für eine Schlange, die sich durch das Gras bewegt. Dieser Ansatz existiert seit langem schon im Comic-Strip, dessen beneidenswert raffinierte Aufteilung zweidimensionaler Bildflächen kurioserweise bei allen Versuchen, Comicfiguren auf Zelluloid zu bannen, ignoriert worden ist zugunsten der öden linearen Erzählweise des starren rechtwinkligen Filmbilds.

NARRATIVE

I am not so sure whether, when compared to the telling of stories with the written word, cinema is such a good narrative medium, especially when cinema is used in its current mimetic, novel-based, literary form. In the cinema, because the telling of the story belongs indisputably to the film-maker, his vision is final, the information he gives is very specific, every emphasis of perspective is determined, the selection and distribution of information are his, and, perhaps most insidiously, the time-frame of the events narrated is his entirely. The contemplation of a viewer before a still image – a painting or a photograph – is dependent on the viewer's time-frame: the *Mona Lisa* can be viewed for four seconds or for four days. Cinema does not permit such space.

The linear pursuit – one story at a time told chronologically – is the standard format of cinema, though some European and Japanese directors have varied the approach to cinematic narrative in ways that anticipate the lateral thinking processes that may soon become commonplace for those educated to think with the CD-ROM as a template. These inventive cinematic efforts have invariably had a literary origin, and if cinema has to take literature as its example, could it not travel on from where Joyce, Eliot, Borges and Perec have already arrived?

There is a general acceptance that cinema is poor at dealing with simultaneity of action. Apart from those occasional two-way telephone conversations viewed by way of a split screen in the 1940s, it has not been cinema's business (as opposed to the theatre) to play two or more activities at once with much conviction. The capture of the imagination of an audience at the theatre or opera is never so rigid or so complete as it is in the cinema. In theatre and opera there are alternative phenomena to watch and listen to: there is simultaneous wide-shot and close-up, action and re-action, foreground and background, the general and the particular all viewable at one and the same time. Is it not possible that cinema can do this successfully as well?

It is true, I think, that we should be heartened by our growing ability to grapple with the new media's tide of information. Shrill and indignant cries of 'visual indigestion' are losing credence, especially among the young

DIE ERZÄHLWEISE

Ich bin mir nicht sicher, ob das Kino – verglichen mit dem geschriebenen Wort – als erzählerisches Medium so geeignet ist, insbesondere die zur Zeit verbreitete, lineare, mimetische, auf Romanen basierende literarische Form des Kinos. Im Kino gebietet der Filmemacher unangefochten darüber, wie eine Geschichte erzählt wird: Seine Vision ist endgültig, die von ihm gegebenen Informationen sind präzise, er entscheidet über Betonungen des Blickwinkels, darüber, was und wieviel er das Publikum wissen läßt; und was vielleicht das Heimtückischste ist: Er hat absolute Kontrolle über den Zeitraum, in welchem die Ereignisse erzählt werden. Wer sich ein unbewegtes Bild – ein Gemälde oder eine Fotografie – betrachtet, bestimmt selbst über den Zeitraum: Die Mona Lisa kann vier Sekunden oder vier Tage lang betrachtet werden. Das Kino läßt uns nicht den Platz dazu.

Das lineare Vorgehen – es wird nur eine Geschichte aufs Mal erzählt, und dies chronologisch – ist das im Kino übliche; doch gewisse europäische und japanische Regisseure haben das filmische Erzählen auf eine Art verändert, die jene laterale Denkweise vorwegnimmt, welche für Menschen, die CD-ROM-gebildet sind, bald selbstverständlich werden dürfte. All diese neuartigen filmischen Leistungen haben literarische Ursprünge. Wenn sich das Kino denn die Literatur zum Vorbild nehmen muß, warum macht es nicht an jenen Punkten weiter, die Joyce, Eliot, Borges und Perec bereits erreicht hatten?

Es ist allgemein bekannt, daß das Kino mit der Gleichzeitigkeit mehrerer Handlungen nur schlecht umgehen kann. Von den gelegentlich in den vierziger Jahren auf einer zweigeteilten Leinwand gezeigten Telefongesprächen abgesehen gab es im Film – im Gegensatz zum Theater – kaum überzeugende Darstellungen von zwei oder mehr Aktivitäten gleichzeitig. Nie wird die Einbildungskraft des Publikums im Theater oder der Oper in so festgelegte, enge Bahnen gelenkt wie im Kino. Im Theater und in der Oper steht fast immer verschiedenes zur Auswahl, dem man zusehen und zuhören kann, dort gibt es gleichzeitig Totalen und Großaufnahmen, können Aktionen und Reaktionen, Vorder- und Hintergründe, Allgemeines und Besonderes alle im selben Moment betrachtet werden. Sollte das Kino dies nicht auch leisten können?

Unsere wachsende Fähigkeit, mit der Flut von Informationsmedien fertigzuwerden, sollte uns ermutigen. Das empörte Geschrei von »visueller Unverdaulichkeit« verliert zunehmend an Glaubwürdigkeit, besonders bei den Jugendlichen, dessen Beherrschung der televisuellen Sprache einen äußerst höhen Grad erreicht hat. Doch was den Film betrifft, mag immer noch was dran sein. Der Grund

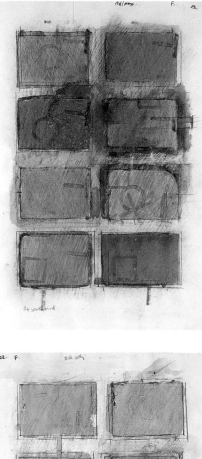

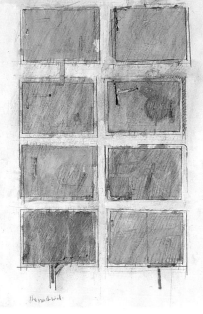

The Circle and the Square, *two details from* A Framed Life *by Peter Greenaway*

Der Kreis und das Quadrat. *Zwei Details aus* Ein gerahmtes Leben *von Peter Greenaway*

whose command of televisual language has become very sophisticated. However, such alarms may perhaps still be valid in the cinema, not because the cinema is incapable of synthesizing large and complex amounts of information, but because its formats and desire for experimentation have too often aimed for the lowest common denominator to fulfil an audience's expectations – saying in effect, we have the control, and you, the viewers, have to fall in line with the film-maker's omnipotence.

It is also true that the film-maker is uniquely blind, for, being invisible to him, an audience's restlessness and irritation are unknown to the film-maker: no immediate change in tack, emphasis or speed is possible. It is too late. Cinema is a one-way traffic: the best that can be hoped is to be able to change the street furniture and the traffic-lights in readiness for the next attempt.

Up against the cinematic barrage that controls so much of the imaginative space, the imagination of the individual receiver is not given much opportunity to re-interpret, re-imagine, re-form, stretch, expand and re-invent the information, and there is no time for a change in individual contemplation, for reassessment, for recapitulation. To lead by the nose is not an ideal way to take advantage of the contribution made by the imagination of an audience, whose capacity to expand and enlarge on such a simple written phrase as 'he opened the door' is going to contain more possibilities than the film-maker can encompass. At present.

dafür ist nicht, daß der Film keine großen Mengen komplexer Informationen verarbeiten könnte, sondern daß formale Vielfalt und Experimentierlust zu oft zugunsten des kleinsten gemeinsamen Nenners aufgegeben und statt dessen einfach die Publikumserwartungen bedient worden sind. Gleichzeitig galt allerdings: »Wir bieten euch den gewünschten Gaumenkitzel, aber wir haben das Sagen, und ihr, Zuschauerinnen und Zuschauer, habt euch der Allmacht des Filmemachers zu beugen.«

Es ist aber auch so, daß der Filmemacher mit einer einzigartigen Form von Blindheit geschlagen ist, denn da er sein Publikum nicht sehen kann, bekommt er nichts von dessen Unruhe und Irritationen mit und sind keine entsprechenden Kurskorrekturen, Akzentverschiebungen und Veränderungen der Tempi möglich. Es ist alles zu spät. Im Kino herrscht Einbahnverkehr: Man kann nur hoffen, die Straßen fürs nächste Mal mit entsprechend anderen Bänken, Papierkörben und Lichtsignalen auszustatten.

Gegen die filmische Sturzflut, die soviel Raum beansprucht, hat die Phantasie der Betrachter kaum eine Chance, die Informationen anders zu interpretieren, sich ein anderes Bild davon zu machen, sie umzuformen, auszudehnen und neu zu erfinden; es fehlt die Zeit für eigene Überlegungen, Einschätzungen, Rekapitulationen. Man führt das Publikum an der Nase herum, statt das auszuschöpfen, was seine Phantasie leisten könnte, die den simplen geschriebenen Satz »Er öffnete die Tür« auf ungleich vielfältigere Weise auszubauen und auszuschmücken vermag, als dies einem Filmemacher möglich ist; zumindest jetzt noch.

AUDIENCE

There is a scene in the film THE BELLY OF AN ARCHITECT where a group of architectural connoisseurs make up an audience to applaud the Pantheon in Rome. They draw up chairs in front of that august building lit by the moonlight and they clap. They applaud heartily. Can architecture be a performance? Can you legitimately applaud a street of buildings? Can you applaud an urban square, a flight of stairs, a statue in the shade of a tree, a group of trees, a city? Is this in fact what we do when we watch a film?

It's been said that the definition of a performance – any performance – is an event that is consciously witnessed by an audience. Such a definition puts the priority of the audience before the performance. To turn any event – from the assassination of dictators to frogs spawning, from sky-diving to leaves falling, from baby-watching to dust-blowing – into performance, all we need is an audience. Maybe events not witnessed by an audience are not only non-performances but non-events.

The standard cinema audience sits passively in the dark mesmerized by the shadows cast by a bright light. Their viewpoint is fixedly in one direction: to the front. But the world is all around us – not just before us. Chair-bound in rows, feet trapped under the seat in front, movement considered a disturbance, we reserve our attention sternly for the flat-screen illusion.

There has been not a little self-congratulation by film-makers on the special sociability of cinema, as though cinema might be offering a unique public service of catharsis, a public-opportunity purgative for privately repressed emotions. But is a visit to the cinema really a community activity in the same way as going to the theatre or going to church or going to a football match? Or even as watching television in a small-audience domestic setting where speech is not banned, movement not

DAS PUBLIKUM

Im Film DER BAUCH DES ARCHITEKTEN gibt es eine Szene, in der eine Gruppe von Architekturkennern sich zu einem Publikum formiert und dem Pantheon in Rom applaudiert. Sie stellen Stühle vor dem erhabenen, vom Mondlicht erhellten Gebäude auf und klatschen begeistert. Kann Architektur eine Darbietung sein? Ist es legitim, einem Straßenzug zu applaudieren, einem städtischen Platz, einer Treppe, einer Statue im Schatten eines Baums, einer Baumgruppe, einer Stadt? Tun wir dies, wenn wir uns einen Film betrachten?

Es wurde gesagt, die Definition einer Performance – jeglicher Darbietung – sei, daß ein Publikum einen Vorgang bewußt verfolge. Eine solche Definition stellt das Publikum über die Darbietung. Um irgendein Ereignis – vom Attentat auf einen Diktator zum Laichen von Fröschen, vom Fallschirmspringen zum Fallen von Herbstblättern, vom Kinderbeaufsichtigen zum Staubwegpusten – zur Darbietung zu erheben, braucht es nichts weiter als ein Publikum. Vielleicht sind Ereignisse, die von keinem Publikum wahrgenommen werden, nicht nur keine Darbietungen, sondern Nichtereignisse.

Das Durchschnitts-Kinopublikum sitzt passiv im Dunkeln, gebannt vom Spiel von Licht und Schatten. Es blickt ausschließlich in eine Richtung, direkt nach vorn. Doch die Welt erstreckt sich um uns herum, sie liegt nicht nur vor uns. An einen Stuhl gefesselt, eingekeilt in eine Sitzreihe, die Füße eingeklemmt unter dem Kinosessel vor uns, so sitzen wir fest, Bewegung wird als störend empfunden, unsere Aufmerksamkeit gilt verbissen einer zweidimensionalen Illusion.

Die Filmemacher haben sich immer mal wieder dazu beglückwünscht, was das Kino für ein Geselligkeit förderndes Medium sei, als biete es Katharsis als öffentliche Dienstleistung, als sei es eine Art kollektives Abführmittel für verdrängte persönliche Gefühle. Doch hat ein Kinobesuch wirklich etwas mit Gemeinschaftsgefühlen zu tun? Wie ein Theaterbesuch, ein Kirchgang oder der Besuch eines Fußballspiels? Oder ein Fernsehabend mit einem kleinen häuslichen Publikum, wo das Reden nicht verboten, die Bewegungs-

The Pantheon and Clapping Audience from The Belly of an Architect

Das Pantheon und das applaudierende Publikum. Aus Der Bauch des Architekten

Audience in The Baby of Mâcon

Publikum. Aus Das Wunder von Mâcon
(Marc Guillaumot)

restricted? Cinema spectators might arrive in crowds and leave in crowds but after the lights go down and whilst the film is active there is an obligation to attend quietly and closely in order to comprehend the unravelling of the film. This seems to suggest that social involvement is severely limited. Could we imagine a cinema where the social activity is increased, where individual time-frames could be adjusted to the freedom of viewing, where there was a possibility for freedom of comparison of views, and no limit, within reason, of private conversation and discourse? Such characteristics are available in the proposition of an exhibition – and isn't cinema an exhibition of sorts, maybe, where the audience moves and not the exhibits? Perhaps we can imagine a cinema where both audience and the exhibits move.

freiheit nicht eingeschränkt ist? Kinogänger kommen und gehen wohl in Gruppen, doch sobald das Licht ausgegangen ist und der Film aktiv wird, ist man verpflichtet, still und aufmerksam zuzusehen, damit man der Entwicklung der Filmhandlung auch zu folgen vermag. Der gesellschaftliche Aspekt ist also äußerst eingeschränkt. Können wir uns ein Kino vorstellen, wo die gesellschaftliche Aktivität größer ist, es dem einzelnen überlassen ist, wie lange er sich etwas betrachtet, wo sich verschiedene Blickwinkel miteinander vergleichen lassen und private Unterhaltungen und Diskussionen in bestimmtem Umfang möglich sind? All diese Eigenschaften treffen auf Ausstellungen zu – ist denn das Kino nicht auch eine Art Ausstellung, in der das Publikum, jedoch nicht die Ausstellungsobjekte sich bewegen? Wäre ein Kino vorstellbar, worin sich Publikum und Ausstellungsobjekte bewegen?

MATERIALITY

Cinema has no intrinsic materiality. This is a statement aggressively rejected as redundant by the *aficionado*, but, I believe, rejected at everyone's peril.

Until the advent of the illusion-at-a-distance medium of film, all established cultural media had, and have, close association with corporeality and physicality, certainly with the corporeality of the creator and frequently with the corporeality of the audience. The body and its hands participate in the manufacture of a painted image and a written word. Three-dimensional space is travelled to participate in the creation of dance and sculpture. Physical energy is generated and dissipated to make music and theatre.

Acknowledgment of stuffs, materials, textures, touch, temperature and the use and manipulation of myriad tools used to be an integral part of the process of creation. In the new TV technologies a need for such corporeality is receding; the scale of concentration at the monitor-screen – the workplace now of image-makers, text-makers, architects, printers, animators, calligraphers, illustrators, film-editors – is intense, and bodily stimulus is very curtailed. The computer mouse now can control everything – even a keyboard for ten fingers is set to become redundant; all work is instigated and executed by one finger and one thumb, and one pair of buttocks fixed to one seat, all in the same location – a location which could be posited practically anywhere without having the slightest effect or influence on the product made.

Cinema as a spectator sport participates in this non-corporeal world – a single-seated-position viewing, eyes front, body fixed. Perhaps it is no accident that cinema's insistence on action within the frame, to the detriment of all else, is increasing. Perhaps it is not coincidental that the representation of bodily contact through the depiction of physical violence and sex is multiplying, while the corporeality of our lives as both creators and spectators is decreasing.

Cinema's low ratio of physicality or corporeality is relevant to the physical relationship it has towards time. History is inimical without respite to film as material. Film as substance gains nothing by becoming old. Film fades,

DIE STOFFLICHKEIT

Das Kino entbehrt jeglicher Stofflichkeit. Diese Aussage wird von den Fanatikern als unwichtig abgetan – zum Schaden aller, wie ich meine.

Alle vor dem »Illusion auf Distanz«-Medium Film entstandenen kulturellen Medien hatten (und haben) einen direkten Bezug zu Körperlichkeit und Dinglichkeit, jedenfalls zur Körperlichkeit des Schöpfers und oft zur Körperlichkeit des Publikums. An der Herstellung eines Gemäldes oder eines geschriebenen Worts sind Körper und Hände beteiligt. Wer etwas auf den Gebieten von Tanz und Skulptur erschafft, bewegt sich im dreidimensionalen Raum. Um Musik und Theater zu machen, bedarf es körperlicher Anstrengung.

Die Kenntnis von Stoffen, Materialien, Texturen, Temperaturen und der Anwendung von Myriaden von Werkzeugen gehörte einfach zum schöpferischen Prozeß. Mit den neuen fernsehtechnischen Möglichkeiten wird das Körperliche immer weniger wichtig. Bei der Arbeit am Monitorbildschirm – der Arbeitsstätte von Bilderproduzenten, Textproduzenten, Architekten, Druckern, Animatoren, Kalligraphen, Illustratoren und Cuttern – ist die Konzentration sehr groß, doch gibt es kaum körperliche Stimuli. Die Computer-Maus macht alles – bald wird auch noch die Zehn-Finger-Tastatur überflüssig werden –, jegliche Arbeit wird von einem Finger und einem Daumen und einem Paar Hinterbacken, die auf einer Sitzfläche kleben, in Angriff genommen und zum Abschluß gebracht; alles geschieht an ein und demselben Ort, wobei es absolut keinen Einfluß auf das Produkt hat, wo dieser sich befindet.

Das Kino als Zuschauersport ist ebenfalls Teil dieser unkörperlichen Welt: Von immer demselben Platz aus sieht man in sitzender Position zu, den Blick nach vorn gerichtet, den Körper unbeweglich am Ort. Vielleicht ist es kein Zufall, daß der Film auf Kosten alles anderen die Aktion mehr und mehr betont und daß mit der Darstellung von Gewalt oder Sexualität immer mehr körperliche Kontakte gezeigt werden, während Körperlichkeit in unserem Leben als Schöpfer und als Zuschauer eine immer kleinere Rolle spielt.

Der geringe Anteil von Stofflichkeit und Körperlichkeit im Kino hat etwas zu tun mit dessen Beziehung zum Faktor Zeit. Dieser ist nämlich für den Film als Material absolut schädlich. Die Substanz Film gewinnt beim Alterungsprozeß absolut nichts. Film verblaßt, verfärbt sich, wird spröde, ist schwierig zu konservieren, und Sonnenschein, Projektion und Transporte sind ihm absolut unzuträglich. Er gewinnt keinen Altersglanz, keine Craquelure Risse, es gibt keine wertvolle Veränderung der Pigmente als Reaktion auf seine

discolours, becomes brittle, is difficult to preserve, suffers by subjection to sunlight, wear, travel. It gains no patina, no craquelure, makes no valuable chemical interaction with its environment, and its requirements for preservation, like its requirements for exhibition, are demanding. It should be preserved by being rolled around itself in metal cans kept at low temperatures and, ideally, in a vacuum. But in preservation ... it is invisible. Without projection machinery to make it manifest, cinema is as nothing.

Unlike architecture or sculpture, theatre or music, a film as substance (as opposed to a film as script) cannot be sensibly photographed or re-photographed for further and alternative interpretation. A film cannot be reworked, though it can be re-made. It cannot profitably be re-framed or re-hung or re-sited or re-written or visually re-translated. Every time you view a film, it is very predictably the same. It is interesting, and significant to this argument, that unlike a church or a house, a gallery or even a museum where other cultural artefacts are presented, the cinema where it shows means virtually nothing to the historical-cultural value of the film shown.

Sedentary, nocturnal, passive, architecturally local, narrative-bound, private-in-public – if these are the conditions of cinema in the 1990s, does it not mean, in the face of so much else that is happening culturally, that the medium and its practitioners are positioned for necessary and urgent renewal?

There is much evidence in the world that, consciously, unconsciously or subconsciously, a negative view of cinema's current sterility of concept and uniformity of execution is strongly enough held to have encouraged people to begin rapidly to do something about it.

Enormous investigation is now underway towards the production of new possibilities of the moving image that will undoubtedly make conventional cinema look very redundant very soon. The dissemination of new technologies for the exploitation of the cinema obsession we have all, in some degree, learnt to live with has begun. After a hundred years cinema is colonizing new aesthetic territory.

Umgebung, seine Konservierung ist aufwendig ebenso wie seine Vorführung. Er bedarf der Konservierung – zusammengerollt in Metallbüchsen bei tiefer Temperatur und idealerweise in einem Vakuum –, doch wenn er konserviert wird, ist er unsichtbar. Ohne eine Projektionsmaschinerie, die ihn sichtbar macht, ist der Film nichts.

Im Gegensatz zu Architektur, Skulptur, Theater oder Musik kann ein bestehender Film (im Gegensatz zu Film als Drehbuch) nicht auf verschiedene Weise fotografiert und interpretiert werden (wie dies die Surrealisten gern mit berühmten Kunstwerken taten). Ein Film läßt sich nicht bearbeiten, er läßt sich nur neu machen als Remake. Er kann nicht umgerahmt, umgehängt, neu situiert, umgeschrieben oder visuell neu umgesetzt werden. Jedesmal, wenn wir uns einen Film ansehen, ist er aller Voraussicht nach gleich, und interessanter- und bezeichnenderweise trägt im Gegensatz zu einer Kirche, einem Haus, einer Galerie oder gar einem Museum, wo andere Kunstschätze präsentiert werden, ein Kino kaum etwas zum kulturhistorischen Wert des Films bei, der darin gezeigt wird.

Sitzend, nächtlich, passiv, architektonisch beschränkt, dem Erzählen verhaftet, in der Öffentlichkeit isoliert – wenn diese Eigenschaften für eine Definition des Kinos der 90er Jahre verbindlich sind, heißt dies nicht (angesichts all dessen, was sonst so kulturell geschieht), daß das Medium und seine Vertreter eine Erneuerung dringend nötig haben?

Sehr vieles deutet darauf hin, daß die Sterilität der Konzepte und die Uniformität der Ausführung im zeitgenössischen Film bewußt, un- oder unterbewußt so negativ empfunden werden, daß jetzt schnell etwas dagegen unternommen werden soll.

Es sind enorme Forschungen im Gange, die zu neuen Formen des bewegten Bildes führen werden, neben denen das konventionelle Kino sehr bald überholt aussehen wird. Eine Unmenge neuer technischer Möglichkeiten zur Ausnutzung jener Filmbesessenheit, mit der wir alle zu leben gelernt haben, ist im Anrollen. Hundert Jahre nach seiner Geburt ist das Kino im Begriff, neues ästhetisches Territorium zu kolonisieren.

THE FIRST FIVE EXHIBITIONS
1. LOCATION AND FRAME – GENEVA

In Geneva, one hundred wooden, white-painted staircases were erected across the city, in major and minor thoroughfares, in parks and public places and along the lake, to provide observation platforms, each with a view-finder, to contemplate one hundred fixed framings of the city – wide shots, medium shots, details. Every site (and sight) was available for viewing day and night for twenty-four hours in all weathers. Since the exhibition lasted a hundred days, it was credible that here were one hundred separate hundred-day-long films with no film in the camera, no possibility of a second take, and with ninety-five per cent of all actions and events being – in normally expected terms of artificial drama – ephemeral. It was certainly true that all actions and events were not predicted or predicated by text.

By night, wherever possible, the chosen site viewed through the staircase view-finder was artificially lit cinematographically to capitalize on its potential drama – through contemplation of its architecture, its detail, its possible entrances and exits, its *genius loci*. It was essential to exploit each site's unreproduceable sense of place. Perhaps the starting point of a contemplation might be the notion that here was a site for a filmable event, but since all events are filmable or, contradictory-wise, unfilmable the notion of cinema being the principal template was variously significant and totally insignificant. Maupassant ironically suggested that all the world exists to be put into a book; perhaps we might now – with increased irony – say that all the world exists to be put into a film.

The results were invigorating. Extreme attention was paid to the limitations and possibilities of the 'artificially framed view' – conclusively emphasizing the frame as a construct, a device, subjectively chosen, as is customary in the constructed drama of cinema and painting. In an attempt to make the content of each 'shot' dictate the framing, the aspect-ratio was changed constantly – a condition rarely encountered when framing cinema; thus notions of manufacturing a wide shot or a detail were possible without using either a wide-angle or a close-up lens, without pushing the landscape further from you, or bringing it artificially closer: a detail seen at a distance remained at a

DIE ERSTEN FÜNF AUSSTELLUNGEN
I. SCHAUPLATZ UND BILDAUSSCHNITT – GENF

In Genf wurden über die Stadt verteilt – an wichtigen und weniger wichtigen Durchfahrtsstraßen, in Parks, auf öffentlichen Plätzen und der Seepromenade – 100 weißgestrichene Holztreppen aufgestellt. Sie waren Beobachtungsstationen, jede mit einem Sucher ausgestattet, durch den sich eine von 100 Stadtansichten betrachten ließ, wobei der Bildausschnitt, die »Kamera-Einstellung« genau festgelegt war: Totale, Halbnahe, Detail. Jede Stätte konnte Tag und Nacht 24 Stunden lang bei jedem Wetter betrachtet werden. Da die Ausstellung 100 Tage lang dauerte, könnte man sagen, daß hier 100 verschiedene 100 Tage lange Filme abliefen, ohne Film in der Kamera, ohne die Möglichkeit eines zweiten Takes, und daß 95% aller Aktionen und Ereignisse dramaturgisch gesprochen ephemerer Natur waren. Auf jeden Fall entsprach keine Aktion und kein Ereignis einem Drehbuch, und mit derselben Bestimmtheit läßt sich sagen, daß keine Aktion und kein Ereignis von einem Text vorausgesagt oder festgelegt worden war.

Wo immer möglich wurden die in den Suchern sichtbaren Sujets nachts kinogerecht ausgeleuchtet, um der Architektur, den Details, den für Auftritte und Abgänge geeigneten Stellen und dem Genius loci ein Maximum an Dramatik abzugewinnen. Es war essentiell, die besondere, nicht reproduzierbare Atmosphäre jeder Stätte hervorzuheben. Vielleicht war der Ausgangspunkt für die Betrachtung einer Stätte die Vorstellung, dies sei der Schauplatz für ein filmbares Ereignis; doch da alle Ereignisse filmbar oder paradoxerweise unfilmbar sind, war die Vorstellung von Film als dem zugrundeliegenden Schema je nachdem wichtig oder völlig unwichtig. Von Maupassant stammt die ironische Formulierung, die Welt sei dazu da, um in einem Buch vorzukommen; vielleicht ließe sich heute mit noch mehr Ironie sagen, die Welt sei dazu da, um in einem Film vorzukommen.

Die Resultate waren erfrischend. Besonders große Aufmerksamkeit galt den Beschränkungen und Möglichkeiten der »künstlich eingerahmten Aussicht«, welche den Rahmen als Konstrukt deutlich machte, als bewußt eingesetzte Vorrichtung, wie man sie aus dem konstruierten Drama von Film und Malerei kennt. Es wurde versucht, den Inhalt jeder »Einstellung« den Rahmen bestimmen zu lassen, wodurch sich die Proportionen ständig änderten – eine Seltenheit, wenn es um den Bildausschnitt im Kino geht; so wurde es möglich, die Vorstellung einer Totalen oder eines Details ohne die Verwendung eines Weitwinkel- oder eines Teleobjektivs zu schaffen, ohne die Landschaft weiter

Location photographs by day and night from THE STAIRS GENEVA

Tages- und Nacht-Fotos von Schauplätzen der Genfer STAIRS

Location photographs by day and night from THE STAIRS GENEVA

Tages- und Nacht-Fotos von Schauplätzen der Genfer STAIRS

distance. On a few occasions, deliberately to disturb the viewer's expectations, the framings were based not on a horizontal but on a diagonal axis – still forming a parallelogram, but with no comforting orthodox horizon. Almost involuntarily this created that search for the horizontal that occurs when, for example, a face is seen upside down in the cinema: heads turn 45°, and more, in an attempt to 'correct' the picture.

Many of the most successful viewpoints in the bright Genevan sunlight were hypnotic in their resolute cropping and cutting of what was considered significant and insignificant – mysteriously heightening the unscripted and apparently ephemeral drama of the streets, often illiciting the surprised response, "But … it is like being in the cinema!" On the other hand, children, very reasonably treating the staircase-framings as a game, but conditioned by their life-training in front of the television set, exclaimed, "But there is nothing there!" – a statement that completely justifies the truism that we have to be taught how to see.

wegzuschieben oder sie künstlich heranzurücken: Ein Detail in der Ferne blieb ein Detail in der Ferne. In ein paar Fällen wurden die Bildausschnitte – um die Erwartungen der Betrachter bewußt zu stören – nicht von der horizontalen, sondern von einer diagonalen Achse ausgehend bestimmt: Sie ergaben Parallelogramme ohne einen beruhigenden orthodoxen Horizont. Diese Situation bewirkte fast zwangsläufig jene Suche nach dem Horizont, die eintritt, wenn im Kino z.B. ein umgedrehtes Gesicht gezeigt wird: Dann drehen sich die Köpfe um 45 Grad und mehr, im Versuch, das Bild zu »korrigieren«.

Viele jener Ausblicke, die im Sonnenlicht besonders lohnend waren, erhielten eine geradezu hypnotische Qualität durch das entschiedene Aussparen und Wegschneiden alles Unwesentlichen und die Konzentration auf das, was als wesentlich erachtet wurde: Die in keinem Drehbuch festgelegten, scheinbar ephemeren Vorgänge auf den Straßen gewannen auf mysteriöse Weise an Dramatik und riefen oft die erstaunte Reaktion »Aber … das ist ja wie im Kino!« hervor. Andererseits riefen Kinder, welche die Treppen mit den Durchblicken als Spielzeug betrachteten, aber von ihrem lebenslangen Training vor den Fernsehern geprägt waren, nachvollziehbarerweise »Aber da ist ja gar nichts!« – eine Aussage, die wieder einmal die Binsenweisheit belegt, daß wir das Sehen erst erlernen müssen.

(opposite) 12 Staircases from THE STAIRS GENEVA

(links) 12 Treppen der Genfer STAIRS

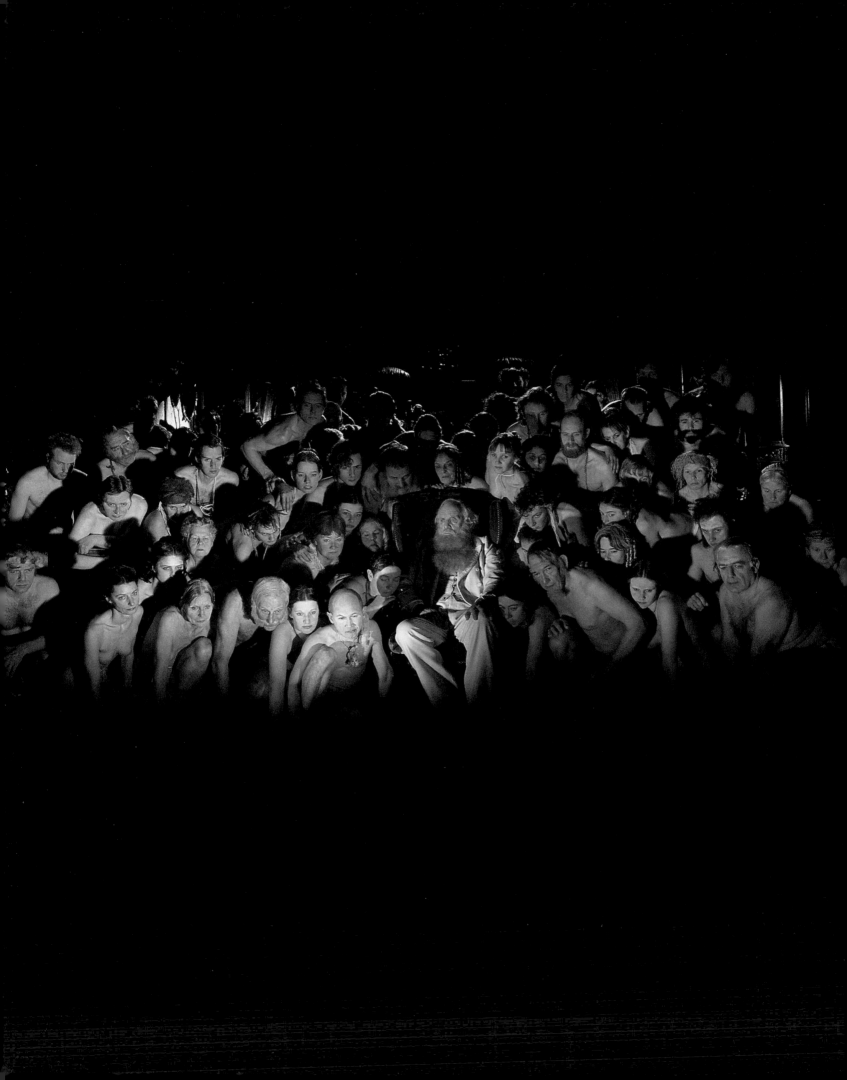

3. THE AUDIENCE – BARCELONA

So many human activities are now accomplished from a sitting position, it might not seem unreasonable for the human body to evolve new anatomical characteristics as important as the changes perfected when the human ape decided to stand. The seat has become the prime article of furniture, from the car to the cinema, the aircraft to the bathroom, the restaurant to the classroom.

At any given moment, a large proportion of the world's population is seated and watching. So much so that the definition of performance given above might be modified: a performance is any event witnessed by a seated audience. Just as, increasingly, we are becoming a planet of spectators hungry for performance, we have also become, willingly or unwillingly, a world of spectators being watched – by the voyeuristic surveillance camera, the domestic camera-recorder, the increasingly intrusive mobile public broadcasting unit. Consider the unknowing 'volunteer' extras viewable nightly in every news broadcast. We could ask, "Who has not been filmed?" – and get no show of upraised hands. We are a world of watchers being watched. We are an audience watching ourselves.

In Barcelona, one thousand numbered seats are to be erected across the city, in various groupings, to create a hypothetical audience for a hundred days, to watch not spectacularly dramatized action, not pre-planned activity, but the everyday life of the city, as though it were a performance viewed from the conventional situation of the theatre stalls or the seat of a stadium or a cinema: the activity of the city as spectacle, as drama, as sport, as education, as entertainment – the five prerequisites of audience attention. A voluntary spectator taking a numbered seat will know that he or she is a potential member of a thousand-seat 'incidental' audience.

It is planned to erect these one thousand seats in public places, in front and inside offices and churches, in hospital grounds, railway stations, airports, in streets and open spaces, cemeteries and schools, before significant and insignificant architectural features, in front of certain statues, billboards and building sites, and also to 'adopt' seats in more officially recognized audience situations, in cinemas, galleries, theatres, race-tracks, bull-rings, sports arenas

3. DAS PUBLIKUM – BARCELONA

So viele menschliche Aktivitäten werden heute in einer sitzenden Position ausgeübt, daß es nicht unvernünftig wäre, wenn der menschliche Körper ebenso wichtige neue anatomische Eigenheiten entwickelte wie damals, als der Menschenaffe auf zwei Beinen zu gehen beschloß. Der Sitz ist zum wichtigsten Möbelstück überhaupt geworden – vom Auto zum Kino, vom Flugzeug zum Bad, vom Restaurant zum Schulzimmer.

In jedem beliebigen Moment ist ein großer Teil der Weltbevölkerung dabei, sich sitzend etwas anzusehen. Die erwähnte Definition einer Darbietung könnte umformuliert werden zu: Eine Darbietung ist ein Ereignis, das von einem sitzenden Publikum verfolgt wird. Und während wir zunehmend zu einem Planeten von Zuschauern werden, die nach einer Darbietung gieren, werden wir gleichzeitig willentlich und unwillentlich zu einer Welt von Zuschauern, die ihrerseits beobachtet werden: von voyeuristischen Überwachungskameras, häuslichen Videorecordern und zunehmend aufdringlichen mobilen Fernsehteams. Denken Sie nur an die nichtsahnenden »freiwilligen« Statisten, die jeden Abend in den Nachrichtensendungen zu betrachten sind. Wir könnten fragen »Wer ist noch nie gefilmt worden?«, ohne daß eine einzige Hand erhoben würde. Wir sind eine Welt von beobachteten Beobachtern. Wir sind ein Publikum, das sich selbst zuschaut.

In Barcelona sollen 1000 numerierte Sitzplätze in verschiedenen Anordnungen über die Stadt verteilt werden, um ein hypothetisches Publikum zu schaffen, das 100 Tage lang zuschaut. Doch es verfolgt keine spektakulär dramatisierten Aktionen, keine geplanten Aktivitäten, sondern das alltägliche Leben der Stadt, als wäre es eine Darbietung, die man normalerweise von einem Stadionssitzplatz, einem Theater- oder einem Kinosessel aus verfolgt: die städtischen Aktivitäten als Spektakel, als Drama, als Sport, als Weiterbildung und als Unterhaltung, womit die fünf Kategorien genannt wären, mit denen das Interesse eines Publikums geweckt werden kann. Wer als freiwilliger Zuschauer auf einem numerierten Sitz Platz nimmt, ist sich bewußt, daß sie oder er einem zufällig zusammengewürfelten tausendköpfigen Publikum angehört.

Es ist geplant, diese 1000 Sitze auf öffentlichen Plätzen zu installieren, vor und in Büros und Kirchen, in der Umgebung von Krankenhäusern, Bahnstationen, Flughäfen, auf Straßen und offenen Flächen, auf Friedhöfen und in Schulen, vor bedeutenden und unbedeutenden Beispielen von Architektur, vor Statuen, Reklamewänden und Baustellen. Es sollen außerdem Sitzplätze an Orten »adoptiert« werden, die auch sonst etwas mit der

Crowd of mourners at Darwin's Funeral from Darwin

Trauergäste bei Darwins Begräbnis. Aus Darwin
(Marc Guillaumot)

Alonso's Banquet in Milan from Prospero's Books

Alonsos Bankett in Mailand. Aus Prosperos Bücher
(Marc Guillaumot)

Audience in the amphitheatre from M is for Man, Music and Mozart

Publikum im Amphitheater. Aus M wie Mensch, Musik, Mozart

(opposite) An Audience from Darwin

(links) Publikum. Aus Darwin
(Marc Guillaumot)

Members of the Cathedral from The Baby of Mâcon

Besucher der Kathedrale. Aus Das Wunder von Mâcon
(Marc Guillaumot)

and football stadia. It is hoped that no activity of a big city will be ignored. An audience at any time may be in a position to see anything – a man taking a dog for a walk, a dog biting a man, a man biting a dog.

Situation des Zuschauens zu tun haben: Kinos, Galerien, Theater, Rennbahnen, Stierkampf-Arenen, Sportplätze und Fußball-stadien. Es ist zu hoffen, daß keine Aktivität einer großen Stadt übergangen wird. Ein jederzeit vorhandenes Publikum ist in der Lage, alles mögliche zu sehen: einen Mann, der einen Hund spazieren führt; einen Hund, der einen Mann beißt; einen Mann, der einen Hund beißt.

(opposite) An Audience of Victorians from Darwin

(rechts) Ein viktorianisches Publikum. Aus Darwin
(Marc Guillaumot)

 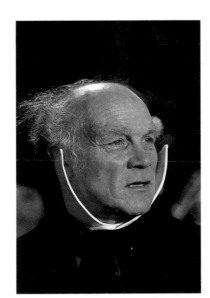 

An audience from Prospero's Magic Island from Prospero's Books

Ein Publikum auf Prosperos Zauberinsel. Aus Prosperos Bücher (Marc Guillaumot)

34

4. 100 ARCHETYPES

The creation of a cast is an act of colonization, like planning a new population for a fictitious world. In the film THE BABY OF MACON, the world was recreated in a theatre audience. In the television documentary DARWIN, the hierarchy of the British Industrial Revolution was re-invented for a battle between Creationists and Darwinists. In the film PROSPERO'S BOOKS, a version of Shakespeare's *The Tempest*, an island was furnished with a representative population that an early seventeenth-century Italian duke and international scholar would recognize. In cinema a crowd is invariably a crowd of representatives: how often the script says, 'a crowd scene'. The crowd scenes are to be watched avidly. And if the planning is good then the crowd may purposefully reprise and complement the principals – making a solid theatre of the world.

Invariably, the members of 'the crowd' are constituted in the same familiar way. In the classroom crowd, there is the fat boy and the wise youth ahead of his years, the comic, the know-all, the coward, the bully, the narcissist, the rabble-rouser and the swot. You may find the same complement in the twelve members of the jury, in the harassed jungle platoon, the prison chain-gang, the office party, the newsroom, the crew of the lost open boat, the abandoned space-ship and the trapped submarine. You'll find them in the cast of parliamentarians brought together to represent democracy. In a cast of kings to represent monarchy. You could probably rework the same archetypes in a cast of severed heads – Louis XVI, Desmoulins, Danton, Robespierre, Charles I, Holofernes, Orpheus, Marie Antoinette, St John, St Denis. Tinker, tailor, soldier, sailor, richman, poorman, beggarman, thief. The cook, the thief, his wife and her lover. In the end, perhaps, all the characters appearing in Western drama can make a recyclable list, a set stock of characters – the unrequited lover, the king and the queen, the knave and the fool, the soldier, the jealous husband, the adventurer, the drunk, the whore and the virgin. Classical mythology has put names to the same archetypes: Orpheus, Jupiter and Juno, Apollo and Marsyas, Mars, Vulcan, Ulysses, Silenus, Circe and Flora; and so has Christianity: Jacob, Solomon and the Queen of Sheba, Judas, Nebuchadnezzer, St George, Potiphar, Joseph, Noah, Mary Magdalene and St Agatha. Characters from celebrated

4. 100 ARCHETYPEN

Die Zusammenstellung einer Besetzung ist ein Akt der Kolonisation, als plante man eine Bevölkerung für eine fiktive Welt. Im Film DAS WUNDER VON MÂCON wurde die Welt in einem Theaterpublikum nachgestaltet. Im Fernseh-Dokumentarfilm DARWIN wurde die Hierarchie der industriellen Revolution in England neu erfunden für einen Kampf zwischen den Darwinisten und den Anhängern der Lehre von der Weltschöpfung durch Gott. Im Film PROSPEROS BÜCHER, einer Interpretation von Shakespeares »Sturm«, wurde eine Insel mit einer repräsentativen Bevölkerung ausgestattet, die ein gelehrter italienischer Herzog des 17. Jahrhunderts erkennen würde. Im Film ist eine Menschenmenge zwangsläufig eine Menge von Repräsentanten. Wie oft steht in einem Drehbuch: »Massenszene«. Es lohnt sich, bei Massenszenen genau hinzusehen. Und wenn die Planung gut ist, sind die Menschen in einer Massenszene eine Wiederaufnahme und eine Erweiterung der Hauptfiguren, wodurch ein komplettes Welttheater entsteht.

Menschenmengen setzen sich immer gleich zusammen: Zur Schulzimmer-Besetzung gehören der dicke Junge, der Frühreife, der Spaßvogel, der Alleswisser, der Feigling, der Tyrann, der Narziß, der Rädelsführer und der Streber. Die gleiche Konstellation findet sich bei Geschworenen, einer Dschungelpatrouille in Bedrängnis, einem Trupp aneinandergeketteter Sträflinge, Bürofesten, in einer Zeitungsredaktion, bei den Insassen eines Rettungsboots, eines aufgegebenen Raumschiffs oder eines festsitzenden U-Boots. Sie findet sich in der Kombination von Parlamentariern, die als Repräsentanten der Demokratie zusammengebracht wurden. In der Kombination von Königen als Repräsentanten der Monarchie. Man könnte wohl die gleiche Besetzung aus abgeschnittenen Köpfen zusammenstellen: Louis XVI., Desmoulins, Danton, Robespierre, Karl I. von Großbritannien, Holofernes, Orpheus, Marie Antoinette, Johannes der Täufer, der heilige Dionysius von Paris. König, Dame, Bube. Der Koch, der Dieb, seine Frau und ihr Liebhaber. Letztendlich ließen sich wohl alle im westlichen Drama vorkommenden Figuren auf einer Liste gängiger Gestalten zusammenstellen: der abgewiesene Liebhaber, der König, die Königin, der Schurke, der Narr, der Soldat, der eifersüchtige Ehemann, der Abenteurer, der Säufer, die Hure und die Jungfrau. Die klassische Mythologie hat diese Archetypen mit Namen versehen – Orpheus, Jupiter, Juno, Pluto, Marsyas, Mars, Vulkan, Odysseus, Silen, Circe und Flora –, das Judentum und das Christentum genauso: Jakob, Salomon, die Königin von Saba, Judas, Nebukadnezar, der heilige Georg, Potiphar, Joseph, Noah, Maria Magdalena und die heilige Agathe. Figuren aus berühmten Werken der Literatur sind

THE FUTURE

The future must be a child with shining eyes and infinite trust. The
Future should be feminine - a black haired girl with blue eyes. There w
a problem - how did the female Future change sex   ome the male
Present   to speak of the male Past?

ABCDEF

33

fiction have become indivisible from their allegorical significance: jealous Othello, handsome Helen, perfidious Richard III, miserly Scrooge, wizardly Faust. Historical characters are exaggerated, maligned or whitewashed to fit the canon: Caesar, Alexander, Columbus, Joan of Arc, Richelieu, Napoleon, Hitler, Churchill. The process does not stop. The demand to re-invent, re-personify the archetype continues.

Perhaps it is still possible to add new creations, like the introduction of the detective and the policeman in the nineteenth century. How about the disc-jockey at the end of the twentieth century? Certainly contemporary cinema has endlessly re-worked the stock-pile – not only within the fictions it portrays, but also out of the actors and actresses it employs to personify them: Madonna and Schwarznegger can perhaps be viewed as variants on the themes of Venus and Hercules, Eve and Samson.

Although a list of archetypes might be conceived in a larger or indeed in a smaller number, one hundred of them have been chosen (in some cases with appropriate variations on the same theme) for consideration, to be re-created by actors and figurants, with all their relevant attributes, props and gestures, in showcases, vitrines and small theatres around the city of the exhibition's choice. The purpose is not only to celebrate the disciplined richness of this consensus collection, but to make connections and associations between the various ways the different media have established these hundred characters, and the limitations that might have ensued in the visual language necessary to identify and exploit them.

untrennbar mit ihrer allegorischen Bedeutung verbunden: der eifersüchtige Othello, die schöne Helena, der hinterlistige Richard III., der geizige Scrooge, der wissensdurstige Faust. Historische Figuren werden verzerrt, verleumdet oder reingewaschen, je nachdem, was in den Kanon paßt: Caesar, Alexander, Kolumbus, die heilige Johanna, Richelieu, Napoleon, Hitler, Churchill. Der Prozeß hat kein Ende. Das Bedürfnis, die Archetypen neu zu erfinden, mit neuen Personen zu identifizieren, hält an.

Vielleicht lassen sich noch Neuschöpfungen hinzufügen wie die Einführung des Detektivs und des Polizisten im 19. Jahrhundert. Wie wäre es mit dem Diskjockey Ende des 20. Jahrhunderts? Das zeitgenössische Kino jedenfalls hat all diese Klischees immer wieder durchgespielt, was nicht nur für die erfundenen Figuren gilt, sondern auch für die Schauspielerinnen und Schauspieler, die diese personifizieren: Madonna und Schwarzenegger können als Varianten von Venus und Eva, Herkules und Samson gesehen werden.

Obschon sich längere, aber auch weitaus kürzere Listen von Archetypen denken ließen, sind in diesem Fall 100 ausgewählt worden (wobei manche von ihnen Abwandlungen desselben Typus sind); sie werden – dargestellt von Schauspielern und Statisten mit all ihren wichtigen Attributen, Requisiten und Gesten – in Schaukästen, Vitrinen und kleinen Theatern überall in der Stadt zu sehen sein, wo die Ausstellung stattfindet. Der Sinn der Sache ist nicht nur, die disziplinierte Fülle dieser Sammlung von Übereinkünften zu feiern, sondern auch aufzuzeigen, wie die verschiedenen Medien diese 100 Figuren geschaffen haben und inwiefern die Identifikation und Ausnutzung dieser Charaktere auch eine Einschränkung der visuellen Sprache bedingt.

(opposite and above) Three Andromaque images from the Strasbourg Book of Allegories

(links und oben) Drei Bilder der Andromache aus dem Straßburger Allegorien-Buch

Still Life and Properties from Prospero's Books

Stilleben und Requisiten. Aus Prosperos Bücher
(Marc Guillaumot)

5. PROPERTIES

There can be few dramas that are successfully performed in the theatre, cinema or in painting that do not have recourse to the significant use of an inanimate object. How many eighteenth-century plays can be performed without a letter and a screen? Is it possible to permit a 1930s American thriller to reach a conclusion without a car, a telephone and a gun? Every Elizabethan prop department had a selection of severed heads and an armoury of daggers. Few Dutch mid-seventeenth-century still-life painters left out a peeled lemon, a lute or a skull. The Victorian melodrama needed a bottle of poison and probably a hangman's noose. It is impossible to imagine Othello without Desdemona's handkerchief, *The Seventh Seal* without a chess-board, *Citizen Kane* without a glass snowstorm, and naturally any drama of Christ's death on stage, screen or canvas without a cross. The treasure-chest in *Treasure Island* becomes the bank-vault in *The Thomas Crown Affair*, the safe-deposit box of *Rififi*, the bullion bags of *Stagecoach*.

How can a drama be invested in an inanimate object? Is it essential that the object implies ownership, or character identity, or does it have worth in some other currency? How often does the inanimate object operate like an attribute in an allegory? Writers must own a typewriter, good wives their wedding-rings, a blindman a white stick, a sunbather dark glasses.

The exhibition of Properties makes a list of one hundred such essential objects that complement the constructed drama of Western culture and then multiplies it by a hundred, each single item being presented with one hundred variations on the same theme as though a choice were available to a props master to select and offer the most appropriate version of a property to complete the drama under his consideration. A case of severed limbs for *Coriolanus*, a chest of daggers for *Julius Caesar*, bottles of ink for writers, one hundred bunches of red roses for desperate lovers, bottles of alcohol for tipplers, one hundred white walking-sticks to demonstrate blindness, one hundred cars stacked and ticketed, their petrol tanks full awaiting the demands of a pursuit. And one hundred small arms, oiled or rusty, primed with bullets or blanks, ready to complete a drama of the Wild West, the First World War, drug-smuggling, Mafia kidnap, domestic violence, suicide or science fiction.

5. DIE REQUISITEN

Kaum ein Drama läßt sich im Theater, im Film oder der Malerei ohne die Verwendung unbelebter Gegenstände darstellen. Wie viele Theaterstücke des 18. Jahrhunderts kämen ohne einen Brief und einen Wandschirm aus? Kann ein amerikanischer Thriller der 30er Jahre ohne ein Auto, ein Telefon oder eine Schußwaffe zum Abschluß kommen? Jeder elisabethanische Requisiteur hatte einen Fundus an abgeschnittenen Köpfen und ein Arsenal von Dolchen. Nur wenige holländische Maler Mitte des 17. Jahrhunderts verzichteten auf geschälte Zitronen, Lauten und Totenschädel. Zu einem viktorianischen Drama gehörte eine Giftflasche und öfter auch der Henkersstrang. Es ist unmöglich, sich »Othello« ohne Desdemonas Taschentuch, das »Siebte Siegel« ohne Schachbrett, »Citizen Kane« ohne Schneekugel und vor allem jegliche Darstellung von Christi Tod in Theater, Film oder Malerei ohne ein Kreuz vorzustellen. Die Schatztruhe aus der »Schatzinsel« wird in »Thomas Crown ist nicht zu fassen« zum Tresorraum, in »Rififi« zum Safe und in »Ringo« zu Säcken voll Gold und Silber.

Wie läßt sich ein lebloser Gegenstand dramatisch aufladen? Ist es wesentlich, daß der Gegenstand etwas mit einem bestimmten Besitzer, dem Charakter einer Person zu tun hat, oder geht es um eine andere Währung? Wie oft funktioniert der leblose Gegenstand wie das Attribut einer Allegorie? Schriftsteller brauchen eine Schreibmaschine, gute Ehefrauen ihre Eheringe, Blinde ihre weißen Stöcke, Sonnenbadende ihre dunkle Brille.

In der Requisiten-Ausstellung werden 100 solche zum konstruierten Drama der westlichen Kultur gehörenden essentiellen Gegenstände aufgelistet und dann verhundertfacht: Von jedem einzelnen Gegenstand werden 100 Varianten präsentiert, als hätte ein Requisiteur aus dem Angebot auszuwählen und das passendste Requisit für ein von ihm betreutes Drama zu liefern. Ein Koffer voll abgeschnittener Glieder für »Coriolan«, eine Kiste voller Dolche für »Julius Caesar«, 100 Sträuße roter Rosen für verzweifelte Liebende, Flaschen voll Tinte für Schriftsteller, Flaschen voll Alkohol für Schluckspechte, 100 weiße Spazierstöcke zur Demonstration von Blindheit, 100 aufeinander gestapelte Autos mit gefüllten Benzintanks und Zetteln, die beschreiben, wofür sie eingesetzt werden, in Erwartung einer Verfolgungsjagd. Und 100 Handfeuerwaffen, frisch geölte und rostige, mit Patronen oder Schreckschußmunition geladen, bereit für ein Wildwestdrama, den Ersten Weltkrieg, eine Drogenschmuggel-Aktion, eine Mafia-Entführung, einen Ehestreit, einen Selbstmord oder eine Science-fiction-Geschichte.

MUNICH – PROJECTION
THE SCREEN AND THE FRAME

The subject of THE STAIRS in Munich is projection.

Cinema is nothing if not a beam of projected light striking a surface with a framed rectangle of brightness into which shadows are introduced to simulate illusions of movement.

Projected light, a frame, a rectangle of brightness, illusions of movement – these are the characteristics of a city-wide exhibition of one hundred screens to be projected on the exterior walls of churches, shopping malls, museums, theatres and public buildings in Munich in the autumn of 1995, the year of the first centenary of cinema.

The shape, proportions, aspect ratio and to some extent scale of the cinema screen on its essential horizontal axis developed from the theatrical stage. The establishment of its format through the efforts of the first exponents of cinema was no doubt influenced by a composite appreciation of cinema's precursors – the so called optical or philosophical toys of the nineteenth century. The connection between the painting frame and the theatre's proscenium arch belongs to a much more distant historical past.

In the long run-up to the 'invention' of cinema, the phenomenon of the persistence of vision, sophisticated geared machinery, and the chemistry of the photographic process had all been known for some time, at least since the 1860s. Edison and his assistant Dickson could be said to have achieved the essentials of cinematic presentation by 1892, by making sympathetic camera and projector mechanisms work to the same common purpose, but the resultant film could only be viewed by looking through a view-finder into a darkened cabinet. Whilst it is curious that the 'cinematograph' patented in 1895 by the Lumière Brothers etymologically stressed movement, the lift-off to true cinematic illusion was made possible by the discovery of how to throw light successfully – to project images. It could be said that artificially projected light is the key to cinema's great public success, because it permits large pictures to be viewed by large audiences.

The sophisticated use of artificial light as a self-conscious manipulative visual tool arrived late. Certainly it arrived

MÜNCHEN – PROJEKTIONEN
DIE LEINWAND UND DER RAHMEN

Thema von THE STAIRS in München ist die Projektion.

Kino ist in erster Linie ein projizierter Lichtstrahl, der auf eine von einem Rahmen begrenzte Fläche ein helles Rechteck wirft, worin Schatten die Illusion von Bewegung zu erzeugen haben.

Projiziertes Licht, ein Rahmen, ein helles Rechteck, Illusion von Bewegung – dies sind die Eigenschaften einer stadtweiten Ausstellung von 100 Leinwänden. Projiziert wird auf die Außenwände von Kirchen, Einkaufszentren, Museen, Theatern und öffentlichen Gebäuden der Stadt München im Herbst des Jahres 1995, da das Kino ein Jahrhundert alt geworden ist.

Form, Proportionen und zu einem gewissem Grad auch die Größe der Kinoleinwand mit ihrer essentiellen waagrechten Achse entwickelten sich aus der Theaterbühne. Als Format trat sie schon mit den ersten Vertretern des Kinos auf den Plan, ohne Zweifel beeinflußt durch die Vorläufer des Kinos, die sogenannten optischen oder philosophischen Spielzeuge des 19. Jahrhunderts. Der Zusammenhang zwischen Bilderrahmen und Bühnenrahmen reicht viel weiter in die Vergangenheit zurück.

Zu der langen Phase vor der »Erfindung« des Kinos gehörten das Wissen um die Nachbildwirkung, die Verfeinerung von Zahnradmechanismen und der Prozeß der Fotografie, die alle mindestens schon seit den 60er Jahren des 19. Jahrhunderts bekannt waren. Man kann sagen, daß Edison und sein Assistent Dickson 1892 die wesentlichen Elemente für eine Filmvorführung beisammen hatten – mit einer Kamera und einem Projektor, die aufeinander abgestimmt waren und demselben Zwecke dienten –, doch mußte der entstandene Film von den einzelnen Zuschauern in einem Guckkasten betrachtet werden. 1895 ließen die Brüder Lumière ihren Cinématographe patentieren. Etymologisch gesehen wird bei dem Wort kurioserweise das Element der Bewegung betont, obschon die wahre filmische Illusion erst mit der Möglichkeit, Licht zu werfen, Bilder zu projizieren, entstand. Die Projektion von Licht und damit die Möglichkeit, großen Zuschauermengen große Bilder zu zeigen, läßt sich mit Fug als der Schlüssel zum großen Publikumserfolg des Kinos bezeichnen.

Die raffinierte Verwendung künstlicher Lichtquellen als gezielt für bestimmte Effekte eingesetzter Kunstgriff ist eine späte Errungenschaft, jedenfalls was die Geschichte der Malerei betrifft. Oft genug war zwar die Wirkung einer einzelnen, nichtsolaren

Location photographs (Ludwigstraße) preparatory to
THE STAIRS MUNICH

Fotos von Schauplätzen (Ludwigstraße) während der Vorbereitung von THE STAIRS *in München*

The Calling of St Matthew *by Caravaggio*

Die Berufung des Matthäus *von Caravaggio*
(San Luigi dei Francesi, Rom)

late in the history of painting. Focussed light from a single, non-solar source had been exercised often enough, but as an emblem, as a symbol, rather than as a practical manifestation – unless the potential of church stained glass is included, which is significant, since the depiction of light as a source was utilized almost exclusively to depict revelation with a religious connotation. Lazarus, Entombments, the Raising of the Dead, Christ's Resurrection and the Harrowing of Hell provide the iconography. An understanding of the value of shadow in modelling painted figures was appreciated by the Romans, but it was a sophistication apparently left underdeveloped in Western art until Giotto. Notwithstanding some isolated exceptions, it was not until other areas of sophistication had entered the painting vocabulary in the sixteenth century that the exploration of artificial light exploded. To offer excuses that artificial light was rare as a phenomenon cannot surely be used to explain the delay. Though a painter would need to light his canvas to see what he was doing, as well as lighting his subject, light by fire, candle and oil-lamp was a steady-state technology. There had been no sudden revelatory improvements. We cannot say that the seventeenth-century

Lichtquelle dargestellt worden, doch als Emblem, als Symbol, nicht als etwas, das zum praktischen Alltag gehörte, es sei denn, wir beziehen die Wirkung der Glasfenster von Kathedralen mit ein, die insofern von Bedeutung ist, als die Darstellung von Lichtquellen fast ausschließlich im religiösen Zusammenhang geschah. Lazarus, Grablegungen, die Erweckung von Toten, Christi Auferstehung und sein Abstieg in die Hölle zur Rettung rechtschaffener Seelen waren die bildlichen Anlässe. Die Römer kannten den Nutzen von Schatten zur Herausmodellierung von Figuren in der Malerei, doch wurde dabei in der westlichen Kunst bis Giotto keine große Raffinesse entwickelt. Es gab ein paar isolierte Ausnahmen, doch erst nachdem andere Finessen in das künstlerische Vokabular der Malerei des 16. Jahrhunderts Eingang gefunden hatten, nahm auch die Auseinandersetzung mit künstlichem Licht explosionsartig zu. Die Verspätung läßt sich gewiß nicht damit begründen, daß künstliches Licht damals ein seltenes Phänomen gewesen sei. Ein Maler mußte nicht nur seine Leinwand beleuchten, um zu sehen, was er tat, sondern auch sein Modell; und Feuer, Kerzen und Öllampen waren technische Errungenschaften, bei denen es keine überraschenden Entwicklungssprünge gab. Man kann nicht sagen, die Tenebristen des 17. Jahrhunderts hätten einer neuen technischen Entdeckung wegen plötzlich so gemalt, während man durchaus sagen kann, Vermeer

Mary Magdalen *by Georges de La Tour*

Maria Magdalena *von Georges de La Tour*
(Musée du Louvre, Paris)

tenebrists suddenly painted as they did because of a new technological discovery, in the way that we can say that Vermeer explored a notion of photographic reality because of the contemporary invention of the *camera obscura*. A Republican Roman would have lit his world much the same way as every succeeding generation until the mid-nineteenth century fossil-fuel exploiters began to turn night into day permanently for all of us.

The celebrated first fully self-conscious example of drama depicted in conditions of artificial light is cited as Raphael's 1517 Vatican Stanze

habe sich als Reaktion auf die zeitgenössische Erfindung der Camera obscura mit photographischem Realismus auseinandergesetzt. Ein Republikaner im alten Rom beleuchtete seine Welt nachts auf ganz ähnliche Weise wie alle nachfolgenden Generationen, bis Mitte des 19. Jahrhunderts die Gaslaterne für alle die Nacht zum Tag machte.

Als erstes berühmtes Beispiel für die selbstzweckhafte Darstellung künstlichen Lichts in einer dramatischen Szene wird Raffaels »Befreiung Petri aus dem Kerker« (1517) in den Vatikanischen Stanzen erwähnt. Das aus häuslichen Situationen bestens vertraute, charakteristisch warme gelb, orange und rote Licht einer brennenden ölgetränkten Fackel

The Origin of Painting *by Joseph Wright of Derby*

Die Entstehung der Malerei *von Joseph Wright of Derby*
(National Gallery of Art, Washington, Paul Mellon Collection)

Liberation of St Peter. The light from a burning oil-soaked brand, characteristically warm – yellow, orange and red – and very familiar from the domestic situation, again becomes the model for the spiritual light of revelation. The projected light shining on Caravaggio's *Calling of St Matthew* is a focussed, hard-edged beam of daylight, but it is modelled on candle-light, and again metaphorically the light of religious calling. The same can be said of the domestic observations and metaphorical significance of the religious paintings of Georges de La Tour. The virtuosity of these tenebrists opened eyes – blasting candle-light through blood-red fingers, dousing horse-flesh in deep flickering shadow, exciting and disturbing us all anew with the erotic potential of firelight on flesh.

Steadily expanding on the tenebrists' example, the nocturnal light of natural phenomena – the erupting volcano, storm lightning, the moon, comets and even the light of the stars – ambitiously entered the painter's vocabulary, and an enthusiast like Joseph Wright of Derby in the eighteenth century made it his entire business, closeted with the new technicians, to render the glint,

wird wieder zum Vorbild für ein spirituelles Licht, das in diesem Fall einen Engel umgibt. Das Licht, das auf Caravaggios Apostel Matthäus fällt, ist ein konzentrierter, klar umrissener Strahl von Tageslicht, doch das Vorbild dafür ist Kerzenlicht, und es handelt sich erneut um die metaphorische Darstellung göttlicher Offenbarung. Das gleiche Prinzip der Beobachtung häuslicher Details und ihrer metaphorischen Umdeutung gilt auch für die religiösen Gemälde von de La Tour. Die Virtuosität dieser Tenebristen öffnete viele Augen: Durch blutrote Finger scheinendes Kerzenlicht, welches das Fleisch von Pferden flackernd in tiefe Schatten taucht, erregt und verstört uns immer neu mit dem erotischen Potential von Feuerschein auf Fleisch.

Als ehrgeizige Weiterentwicklung des Vorbilds der Tenebristen fand das nächtliche Licht von Naturphänomenen – der ausbrechende Vulkan, Blitze im Sturmgewitter, der Mond, Kometen und sogar das Licht der Sterne – Eingang in das Vokabular der Malerei, und ein Enthusiast wie Joseph Wright of Derby, der gern mit den Vertretern der neuen Technik zusammensteckte, machte es sich im 18. Jahrhundert zur Aufgabe, das Glitzern, Schimmern, Funkeln und Blitzen von künstlichem Licht auf allen möglichen Metallen, Oberflächen und Texturen wiederzugeben.

shine, glisten and glow of artificial light on every metal, surface and texture he could lay his hands on.

Joseph Wright, in keeping with the characteristics of his reputation as an 'industrial tenebrist', and because it offered a comment on his profession, painted a version of *The Origin of Painting*: a young woman of Corinth, anxious about the departure of her lover, traces the silhouette of his shadow on a wall as a remembrance of his true likeness. A shadow on a wall. A true likeness. The fixing of shadows. A remembrance. Perhaps there could not be a more suitable iconography to begin the history of cinema as well as the history of painting.

As an acknowledgement to the representation of the shadow without which no creature under the sun except the devil can exist, the first exhibit in the Vienna exhibition 100 OBJECTS TO REPRESENT THE WORLD was just that – a shadow made by the viewer himself stepping into the darkness of the exhibition space as though stepping into a darkened cinema, waiting, hoping, for the film-maker-lover to fix it eternally.

It has been said that photography was the best thing that could have happened to painting. After the first years of hectic imitation, painting, suffering in the public eye a new inferiority complex about verisimilitude and notions of truthfulness to life, began to free itself of the responsibilities of narration, and the drudgery of documentation. After 1895, was the cinema also responsible for a similar re-evaluation? It is possible to see that notions of slow motion, speeded-up motion, soft focus, superimposition – all easily achievable in cinema – have intrigued painters in the early decades of the twentieth century, but the observable characteristics of light accentuated in the moving photographic image had a more persuasive general effect: De Chirico's silent shadows, Eduard Hopper's light-dominated interiors, Balthus's erotic tableaux indicate painters coming of age with cinema, their lives and work running parallel. The cinema itself, with irony and amusement, also plays the imitative game on itself, making cinematic references to its own passion for the power and illusion of the projected beam of light: the cinema audiences rapt in attention beneath the smoke-filled projector-beam in more than one Fellini film, the shadow-play in Wenders's *Kings of the Road*, the

Passend zu seinem Ruf als »Tenebrist der Industrie« und gleichzeitig als Kommentar zu seinem Beruf malte Joseph Wright seine Version von »Die Entstehung der Malerei«. Wie Plinius berichtet, hielt eine junge Frau aus Korinth, der es vor der bevorstehenden Abreise ihres Geliebten bangte, die Umrisse von dessen Schatten an der Wand fest, zur Erinnerung an sein wahres Aussehen. Ein Schatten an einer Wand. Das wahre Aussehen. Das Dauerhaftmachen eines Schattens. Eine Erinnerung. Vielleicht ist das überhaupt die passendste Ikonographie für den Beginn der Geschichte des Films wie der Geschichte der Malerei.

Als Würdigung des Schattens, ohne welchen außer dem Teufel kein Wesen unter der Sonne existieren kann, war das erste Objekt der von mir in Wien organisierten Ausstellung 100 OBJEKTE ZEIGEN DIE WELT eben dies: Ein Schatten, der von den Besucherinnen und Besuchern geworfen wurde, bevor sie in die Dunkelheit des Ausstellungsraumes traten wie in die Dunkelheit eines Kinos in der Erwartung, Hoffnung, der Filmemacher-Liebhaber werde den Schatten für die Ewigkeit festhalten.

Es ist gesagt worden, die Fotografie sei das Beste, was der Malerei habe passieren können. Während der ersten Jahre hektischer Imitation entwickelte die Malerei in Hinblick auf Realität und Lebensechtheit dem Publikum gegenüber einen neuen Minderwertigkeitskomplex; doch dann befreite sie sich von den Verpflichtungen des Erzählerischen, der Plackerei des Dokumentarischen. Läßt sich sagen, das Kino habe nach 1895 eine ähnliche Neubestimmung ausgelöst? Es läßt sich nachweisen, daß Ideen wie Zeitlupe, Zeitraffer, Weichzeichnung, Doppelbelichtung – die alle im Film sehr leicht zu verwirklichen sind – die Maler der ersten Jahrzehnts interessiert haben, doch die im bewegten fotografischen Bild akzentuierten und isolierten Eigenschaften von Licht hatten eine breitere und nachhaltigere Wirkung: De Chiricos stumme Schatten, Hoppers von Licht dominierte Interieurs, die erotischen Tableaux eines Balthus verraten Maler, die mit dem Kino großgeworden sind, deren Leben sich parallel dazu entwickelt hat. Auch das Kino bespiegelt, ironisch und amüsiert, sich selbst und seine Leidenschaft für die Macht und die Illusion des projizierten Lichtstrahls: in mehr als einem Film von Fellini das entrückte Publikum unter dem von Rauchschwaden erfüllten Projektorstrahl, die Schattenspiele in Wenders' »Im Lauf der Zeit«, das schwankende Licht des Projektors auf der Suche nach seiner Leinwand in Tornatores »Cinema Paradiso«, Godards Amateursoldaten, die in »Die Karabinieri« den Rand der Leinwand aufheben, um zu sehen, wohin die Handlung entschwunden ist, Woody Allens Hommage an den illusionären und

Shadows from the Vienna exhibition 100 Objects to Represent the World

Schatten aus der Wiener Ausstellung 100 Objekte zeigen die Welt
(Manu. Luksch)

Installation from the Rotterdam exhibition The Physical Self

Installation aus der Rotterdamer Ausstellung Das körperliche Ich
(Peter Cox)

swaying projector searchlight searching for its screen in *Cinema Paradiso*, Godard's amateur soldiers lifting up the edges of the screen to understand where the action has gone in *Les Carabiniers*, Woody Allen's homage to the illusion and deceit of the projector-beam's magic in *The Purple Rose of Cairo*.

The abandoned lover in Joseph Wright's *The Origin of Painting* – which we can now also, with a little license, call *The Origin of Cinema* – was a potter's daughter. Appro-priately, Wright's version was intended for his friend Josiah Wedgwood. Later versions of the story suggest that to comfort his abandoned daughter further, her potter father filled in and rounded out the silhouette of the lover's face on the wall with clay. And subsequently baked it. Could this be a curious prophetic foretaste of the future of cinema? The three-dimensional quality is certainly possible, but solid, palpable, physical? Bakeable? Ceramic films? Pots are among the world's oldest artefacts: they have endured for 30,000 years. Could one hope for such an endurance from cinema?

betrügerischen Zauber des Projektorstrahls in »The Purple Rose of Cairo«.

Die Liebende in Joseph Wrights »Entstehung der Malerei« – wir nehmen uns die Freiheit, es nun auch die »Entstehung des Kinos« zu nennen – ist die Tochter eines Töpfers. Wrights Bild war denn auch für seinen Freund Josiah Wedgwood bestimmt. Späteren Versionen der Geschichte zufolge füllte der Vater, der seine verlassene Tochter so gut wie möglich trösten wollte, die Silhouette des Gesichts des Geliebten mit Ton und modellierte es heraus. Danach buk er es. Ist dies vielleicht ein seltsam prophetischer Vorgeschmack auf die Zukunft des Kinos? Dreidimensional, das liegt auf jeden Fall im Bereich des Möglichen. Aber fest, dinglich, greifbar? Backbar? Keramik-Filme? Töpfe gehören zu den ältesten Kunstwerken der Welt, sie haben bis zu 30 000 Jahren überdauert. Darf man hoffen, daß das Kino so lange überdauert?

Seit langem schon fasziniert mich die Idee der Leinwand als solcher, dieser weißen, abgetrennten, die Aufmerksamkeit bündelnden Arena, dieses genau umrissenen Bereichs der Projektion, dessen Reflexionsfähigkeit so essentiell für die gute Sichtbarkeit eines Films ist. Ich komponiere Bilder für eine ganz bestimmte Leinwandfläche, deren Begrenzung

From the series A Framed Life *by Peter Greenaway*

Aus der Serie Ein gerahmtes Leben *von Peter Greenaway*

I have long been fascinated with the idea of the screen itself, the white, focussed, roped-off arena of attention, the legitimized area for projection which is quite precise and of which the reflective potential is so essential for the film to be seen well. I make a very conscious screen-space image where the edges of the composition are important. Taking lessons from the discoveries of twentieth-century painting I am very conscious of the screen edge, the thin harsh line that should ideally make a sharp division between bright light and utter darkness. In cinema this screen edge is not always dependable. It shifts and moves. Due to the vagaries of cinema equipment, of cinema furniture and of care of the projector, it can be soft, wide, indeterminate, coloured, rainbow-hued, round-cornered or otherwise multiply distorted. I am troubled by projectionists who are cavalier about the cinema rectangle so that the projection spills over into the surround, so that the correct projection area is not respected, so that the light levels are incorrect and uneven across the screen. Having seen films in all stages of their manufacture, as test-prints, rushes, viewing prints and projection prints, shown under all manner of screen presentation in many countries for many years, I am only too aware that the film-maker's last collaborator is the projectionist.

Maybe it was these anxieties that led to

wichtig ist. Ich habe von den Erkenntnissen der Malerei des 20. Jahrhunderts gelernt und bin mir sehr bewußt, wo die Begrenzung der Leinwand verläuft, diese dünne Linie, die im Idealfall eine scharfe Trennung zwischen hellem Licht und völliger Dunkelheit darstellen sollte. Doch im Kino ist auf diese Begrenzung der Leinwand kein Verlaß. Ungenauigkeiten bei der Ausrüstung und der Installation von Kinos und mangelnde Pflege der Projektoren führen dazu, daß diese Grenze verschwommen, breit, unklar, bunt, regenbogenfarbig, abgerundet oder sonstwie verformt ist. Ich habe zu kämpfen mit Filmvorführern, denen das Bildformat egal ist, bei denen das projizierte Licht auch noch auf die Umrandung fällt, der korrekte Projektionsbereich nicht respektiert wird, die Helligkeit nicht stimmt und ungleich über die Leinwand verteilt ist. Nachdem ich meine Filme in allen Stadien ihrer Herstellung – Probekopien, Muster, Arbeitskopien und Kinokopien – und im Lauf von zwanzig Jahren in allerlei Ländern auf alle möglichen Arten projiziert gesehen habe, ist mir nur zu bewußt, daß der letzte Mitarbeiter eines Filmemachers der Filmvorführer ist.

Vielleicht sind diese Sorgen der Grund dafür, daß ich in der Serie *Ein gerahmtes Leben* die Leinwand immer wieder mit Farbe auf Papier geschaffen habe. Oft habe ich dabei ein dem Storyboard ähnliches Format verwendet – ein Blatt mit acht Bildern, gleich großen Rechtecken, die auf einer Seite symmetrisch verteilt werden. Sie haben meistens etwas gemeinsam – Grundfarben, die gleiche Textur – und wirken auf die Netzhaut nach dem

Prinzip des Nachbilds, indem das ruhelose Auge von links nach rechts, hinauf und hinunter, vorwärts und rückwärts schweift, und so der Eindruck von Bewegung entsteht.

Im Kino gibt es nur eine Blickrichtung – nach vorn –, hier haben wir die Freiheit, uns in verschiedene Richtungen zu bewegen, wahrscheinlich nicht nur räumlich, sondern auch zeitlich. Das Auge glaubt entweder, daß es eine Bewegung gibt – wie bei einem Daumenkino, einer Fotosequenz von Muybridge oder Marey, einem Comic-strip oder eben einer Filmsequenz –, oder dann glaubt es, daß alle acht Rechtecke einer Sequenz das gleiche Rechteck sind, und produziert so ein einziges achtfach überlagertes Bild von großer Komplexität.

Das Format eines auf die Leinwand projizierten Bildes steht zwangsläufig in einem bestimmten Verhältnis zum Format des Bilds auf dem Filmstreifen einerseits und dem Sucher der Kamera andererseits. Heutzutage sind die verschiedensten Permutationen möglich, je nach Filmformat – 16 mm, 35 mm, 70 mm, super-16 mm, super-35 mm – und je nach Linsen, da sich mit Hilfe anamorphotischer Verzerrung ja ein Pseudo-70-mm-Breitwandfilm mit 35-mm-Material drehen läßt. Seither sind die Verhältnisse von Leinwand, Filmbild und Sucher zueinander nicht mehr so unkompliziert. Dies wurde besonders deutlich, wenn bei den Dreharbeiten zu DER KONTRAKT DES ZEICHNERS eine Einstellung durch den vom Zeichner verwendeten Visierapparat gefilmt wurde. Zunächst war es technisch schwierig, den vom

45

Still from The Draughtsman's Contract

Aus Der Kontrakt des Zeichners

An Artist drawing a Woman using an Optical Frame *by Dürer*

Künstler, eine Frau unter Verwendung eines Visierapparat zeichnend *von Dürer*

repeated manufacture and depiction of the screen on paper in the *Framed Life* series. The format used is related to the discipline of the storyboard, and in my case that means a sheet of eight images, eight rectangles of the same size arranged symmetrically on a page. They usually have a common characteristic, or a common colour-base, or a common shared texture, and they work on the retina by persistence of vision, in which the restless eye moves from left to right, up and down, back and forth across the frames so that a suggestion of animation results. In the cinema the persistence of vision works all one way: forwards. There is freedom here to work in different directions and possibly, by inference, in different tenses. The eye believes either that there is movement – as in a flick-book, a Muybridge photographic sequence, a Marey multiple-image sequence, or a *bande dessinée* – or that all eight rectangles in one sequence are the same rectangle, producing a single, times-eight superimposed image of great richness.

The aspect ratio of a projected screen image must have some relationship with the frame of film on the emulsion strip and with the viewing-gate in the camera. Nowadays, with various permutations possible according to the choice of stock (16 mm, 35 mm, 70 mm, super-16 mm, super-35 mm), and according to the use of lenses through which, anamorphically, it is possible to shoot a fake 70mm Cinemascope on 35 mm, the relationships between screen, frame and viewing-gate are not so straightforward. This was especially proven to be true and graphically illustrated when the optical device of THE DRAUGHTSMAN'S CONTRACT was employed to make a frame. Initially it was technically difficult to make an alignment between what the optical

device framed and what the camera framed, because the human lens is infinitely adjustable and rarely fixed at one viewing distance. But there was a greater difficulty. Dürer and Canaletto certainly used a drawing frame, which could be defined as an invisible screen employing the use of a back projection supplied by nature, but, despite appearances, it is not quite the useful apparatus it appears to be. Human vision is binocular, and the head moves – two characteristics which the camera and the screen do not imitate, however we may wish to simulate them by some form of three-dimensional illusion or a moving camera. Did Dürer and Canaletto know about the persistence of vision, and if not, did their ignorance help rather than hinder their efforts? Could they indeed have conceived the idea of a projected image that threw its light back at the viewer?

I have never ceased to worry at these and many more questions relating to the projection format of film and the presentation format of painting, and have found it impossible to acquiesce in a tradition that seeks to naturalize or take as given the fundamental artificiality of the frame on screen.

Visierapparat eingerahmten und den von der Kamera eingerahmten Bildausschnitt zur Deckung zu bringen, denn die menschliche Linse ist unendlich anpassungsfähig und kaum je auf eine einzige Distanz fixiert. Doch es gab noch eine größere Schwierigkeit. Dürer und Canaletto hatten beide mit einem Visierapparat gearbeitet, den man als unsichtbare Leinwand mit einer von der Natur gelieferten Rückprojektion definieren könnte, doch er war kein so nützliches Hilfsmittel, wie man auf den ersten Blick erwarten würde, denn der Gesichtssinn des Menschen ist binokular und der Kopf beweglich – zwei Eigenschaften, die der Kamera und der Leinwand abgehen, auch wenn wir sie durch die Illusion von Dreidimensionalität und eine bewegte Kamera zu simulieren versuchen. Übrigens: Wußten Dürer und Canaletto um die Nachbildwirkung, und wenn nicht, war ihre Ignoranz bei ihren Bestrebungen eher nützlich als hinderlich? Hätten sie sich ein projiziertes Bild vorstellen können, das sein Licht auf den Betrachter zurückwirft?

Diese und viele weitere Fragen im Zusammenhang mit dem Projektionsformat von Filmen und dem Präsentationsformat von Gemälden haben mich unablässig beschäftigt, und es hat sich für mich als unmöglich erwiesen, mich einer Tradition zu fügen, die versucht, die grundsätzliche Künstlichkeit eines Rahmens oder der Leinwand als natürlich zu erklären oder als gegeben hinzunehmen.

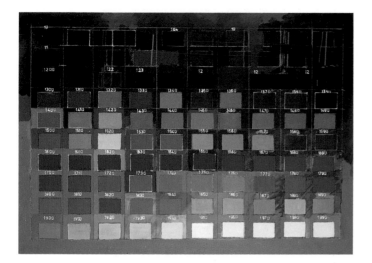

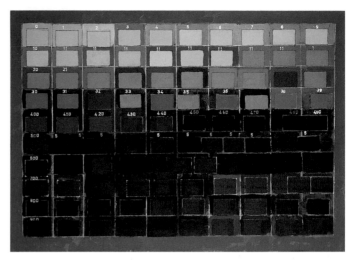

A frame for Byzantium by Peter Greenaway

Ein Rahmen für Byzanz *von Peter Greenaway*

(top left) To the Millennium *by Peter Greenaway*

(oben links) Zur Jahrtausendwende *von Peter Greenaway*

(top right) Schweeger's Frames *by Peter Greenaway*

(oben rechts) Schweegers Rahmen *von Peter Greenaway*

PRELIMINARY EXPLANATIONS

Relative to a project of one hundred projection screens in Munich, and also to a still larger scheme celebrating one thousand years of a more general history – for I was even worried that the frame would become obsolete before its dominance over representation had been adequately acknowledged – I tried, as a schematic approach, to organize the technological history of the projection screen in a series of diagramatic works on paper, feeling free to adapt the scheme where necessary to avoid tedious repetition and to take advantage of the vagaries of the paint surface and colour.

Nevertheless the overall scheme employed for the Munich screens is relatively simple, dividing the technical history of cinema into five broad areas corresponding to developments in the aspect ratio of the screen, the introduction of colour and sound, the advent of television, and the immediate effect television had in persuading the cinema to expand its screen potential.

It was considered very desirable at one stage to try to make these screens have a daytime presence in the city, but the concept of an unlit screen is curiously contradictory, and in the face also of considering how, inexpensively, to manage the daytime screen-construction without harming, hiding or otherwise disturbing the architectural fabric of the city, that part of the project was thankfully abandoned. Besides, who watches a screen without its projected image? Who indeed sits in the lit auditorium of a cinema without feeling a sense of dejection and disappointment?

VORBEREITENDE FORSCHUNGSARBEITEN

Im Zusammenhang mit dem Projekt der 100 Leinwände in München und in Hinblick auf tausend Jahre allgemeinerer Geschichte (ich befürchtete schon, der Rahmen könnte sich überlebt haben, bevor überhaupt wahrgenommen würde, wie sehr er bildliche Darstellungen dominierte) habe ich die technische Entwicklung der Kinoleinwand schematisch in eine Reihe von Diagrammen auf Papier zu gliedern versucht, wobei ich mir vom Schema abzuweichen erlaubte, wenn es zu langweiligen Wiederholungen geführt hätte, und dem Spiel von Oberfläche und Farben freien Lauf ließ.

Dennoch ist das allgemeine Schema relativ einfach: Die technische Entwicklungsgeschichte des Kinos wurde in fünf grobe Bereiche aufgeteilt, die zu tun hatten mit der Entwicklung des Bildformats, der Einführung von Farbe und Ton, dem Aufkommen des Fernsehens und dessen direkten Folgen für das Kino, welches daraufhin die Vorteile der großen Leinwände auszuspielen beschloß.

Es gab eine Phase, in der es wünschbar schien, diese Leinwände auch tagsüber in der Stadt präsent sein zu lassen. Doch die Vorstellung einer nicht beleuchteten Leinwand hat etwas seltsam Widersprüchliches, und weil es überdies unmöglich schien, die Leinwände mit billigen Mitteln tagsüber sichtbar zu machen, ohne die architektonische Substanz der Stadt zu beschädigen, zu verdecken oder sonstwie zu stören, wurde auf diesen Aspekt des Projekts glücklicherweise verzichtet. Außerdem: Wer sieht sich eine Leinwand ohne ein darauf projiziertes Bild an? Wer sitzt im hellen Zuschauerraum eines Kinos ohne ein Gefühl der Enttäuschung und der Niedergeschlagenheit?

ORGANIZATION OF THE MUNICH SCREENS

The ambition of the Munich exhibition is to light up the city at night with the light of one hundred screens, one screen for each year of the hundred years of cinema. It was initially intended to spread the location of the screens wide across the city and out into the suburbs, the sites being chosen to maximize the attention of a potential ambulatory audience. But whereas the people of the suburbs are likely at some stage to come into the centre of the city, the opposite is not necessarily true, so a decision was taken to concentrate the screens in the centre of the city in an area from St. Jakobsplatz to the Haus der Kunst and from the Königsplatz to the river. It is a large, but not too large, area to be walked comfortably by an industrious pedestrian in some three hours, say the length of an evening.

The event was fixed relative to a date that would maximize the dark hours that could still be considered comfortable to a pedestrian walking in the city, that is, in October, from six o'clock in the evening until midnight.

No attempt whatsoever has been made to introduce figuration into the projections. First, it would make the act of projection anecdotal, and it would set up questions that are not addressed here, for if one hundred screens are to be represented – one for each year of cinema – which moving images (and not individual still frames) would have to be chosen? Decisions could only be made on subjective grounds, thus condemning them as unrepresentative. Even if some common consensus opinion prevailed, I suspect that areas of interest associated with nostalgia, nationalism or popularity would cloud the purpose, and these three criteria, in the end, are a very unsure indication of worth.

This, therefore, is to be an installation of screens: a manifestation of one hundred non-figurative projections to celebrate the act of light projection as the dominant characteristic of cinema. Simulation of the actual movement of the moving image is to be undertaken by means that will be associated with the mechanisms of camera and projector, with the notion of the colouring of shadows and a nod to those optical devices of wipe and mix that have long been employed by cinema.

ORGANISATION DER MÜNCHNER LEINWÄNDE

Ziel der Münchner Ausstellung ist, die Stadt nachts mit dem Licht von 100 Leinwänden zu erhellen, einer Leinwand für jedes Jahr seit dem Bestehen des Kinos. Ursprünglich sollten die Leinwände über die ganze Stadt bis hinaus in die Vororte verteilt und die Standorte so ausgewählt werden, daß sie bei dem potentiellen Publikum von Spaziergängern möglichst viel Aufmerksamkeit erregten. Doch während die Menschen aus den Vororten öfter mal in die Stadt kommen, ist das Umgekehrte nicht unbedingt der Fall, und so wurde beschlossen, die Leinwände auf einen Bereich im Zentrum der Stadt zu konzentrieren, der vom Sankt-Jakobs-Platz zum Haus der Kunst und vom Königsplatz bis zur Isar reicht. Dies ist ein großes, aber nicht zu großes Gebiet, das sich von einem emsigen Fußgänger in rund drei Stunden, also der Länge eines Abends, bequem abschreiten läßt.

Das Datum des Anlasses im Oktober wurde so gewählt, daß es möglichst lang vor Mitternacht – gegen 18 Uhr – dunkel würde, Wetter und Temperaturen aber noch erträglich wären.

Es wurde keinerlei Versuch gemacht, figurative Elemente in die Projektionen einzubringen. Zum einen würde dies die Sache anekdotisch machen, zum andern eine Menge Fragen aufwerfen, um die es hier nicht geht, denn wenn wir 100 Leinwände zur Repräsentation des Kinos haben, welche bewegten Bilder (nicht Standbilder) müßten dann für jedes der 100 Jahre ausgewählt werden? Die Entscheidungen fielen gezwungenermaßen subjektiv aus, wodurch sie unrepräsentativ würden. Setzte sich hingegen eine übereinstimmende Meinung durch, so vermute ich, daß das Bild durch Nostalgie, Nationalismus und Popularität getrübt würde, Kategorien, die als Gradmesser für den eigentlichen Wert einer Sache ausgesprochen unzuverlässig sind.

Geplant ist also die Installation von Leinwänden mit 100 nichtfigurativen Projektionen zur Feier des Aktes der Projektion als Hauptcharakteristikum des Kinos. Die Simulation eines bewegten Bildes wird mit Mitteln erreicht, die mit der Mechanik von Kamera und Projektor zu tun haben, mit farbigen Schatten und jenen optischen Mitteln wie Wischblende und Doppelbelichtung, die im Kino seit langem gang und gäbe sind.

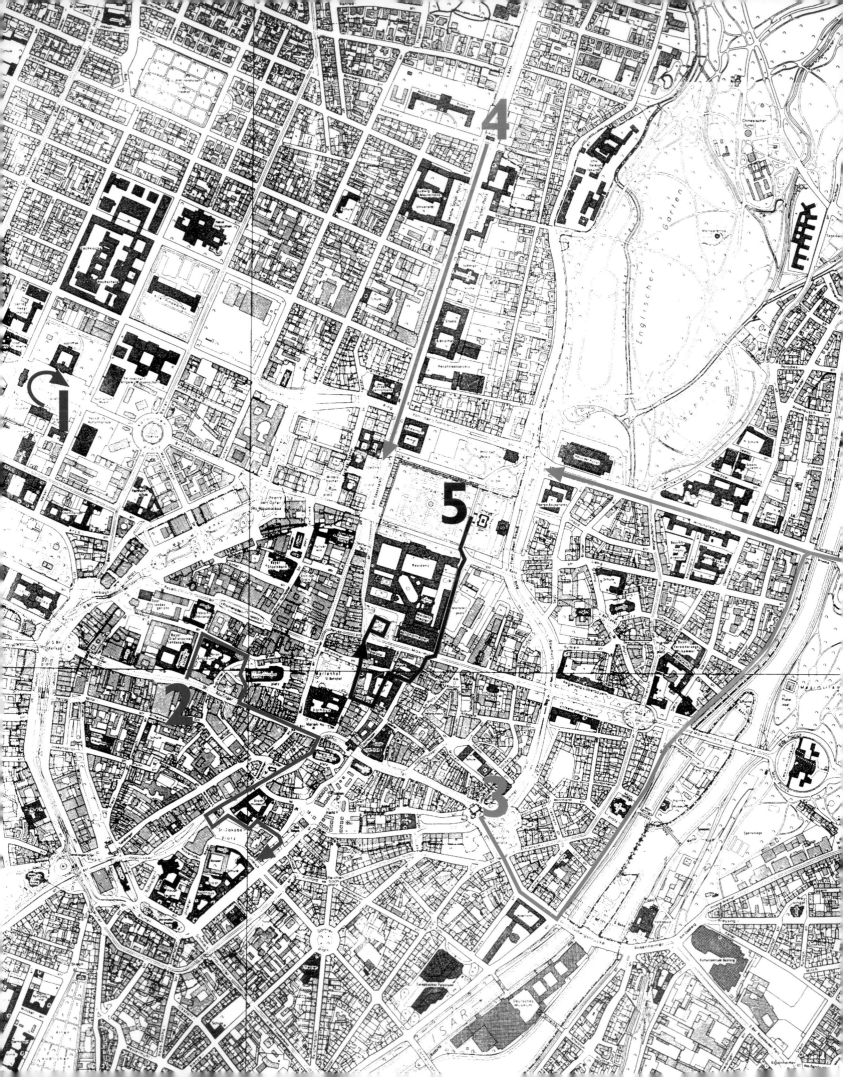

The strong beam of projected light with its moving shadows is to be the predominant image of the screen-space, oblivious of the interruption of window and cornice, brick, stone, tile or cement-rendering – creating a rectangle with pronounced edges. Inside the magic illuminated rectangle is cinema, outside is nothing and the night.

For our present purpose, in technological terms, the history of the cinema as an art of light projection is to be divided up into five sections.

1. 1895 to 1935
Early cinema projection which is predominantly black and white and has a boxy ratio around the region of 1 to 1.33, the present aspect ratio of the television screen.
2. 1936 onwards
The advent of colour.
3. 1946 onwards
The advent of TV.
4. 1953 onwards
The advent of Cinemascope and other related ratios in reaction to the introduction and characteristics of television.
5. 1970 onwards
The new developments in Imax and Omnimax.

These characteristics are represented with the hundred screens in Munich, though scrutiny of cinema history soon reveals that in detail many of these factors may overlap. For example, though early cinema is characteristically black and white, there were experiments in colour-tinting the film frame after it has been printed, and in the 1930s there was some investigation into a process of pre-colouring the stock in the laboratory before the film was exposed in the camera. After the establishment of colour as standard procedure, many films deliberately used black and white for reasons of economy or from deliberate aesthetic choice. Television was available to the scientist and to the wealthy before 1946. Abel Gance in the late 1920s was successfully developing a wide-screen format by expanding his film-screen potential sideways and duplicating or triplicating his film area.

Der starke Strahl projizierten Lichts mit den sich darin bewegenden Schatten soll das dominierende Bild innerhalb der Projektionsfläche sein – egal ob diese unterbrochen wird durch Fenster und Friese, Backsteine, Steine, Klinker oder Zement – und ein scharf umrissenes Rechteck schaffen.

Innerhalb des magisch beleuchteten Rechtecks ist Kino, außerhalb ist Nacht, ist nichts.

Für unsere Zwecke wird die Geschichte des Kinos als Kunst der Projektion von Licht nach fünf technischen Aspekten aufgeteilt:

1. 1895–1935
Frühe Filmprojektion, vorwiegend schwarzweiß und mit einem Bildformat von ungefähr 1 : 1,33, was den gegenwärtigen Proportionen eines Fernsehbildschirms entspricht.
2. Ab 1936
Das Aufkommen des Farbfilms.
3. Ab 1946
Das Aufkommen des Fernsehens.
4. Ab 1953
Das Aufkommen von Cinemascope und verwandten Bildformaten als Reaktion auf die Eigenschaften des neu eingeführten Fernsehens.
5. Ab 1970
Die Entwicklung der übergroßen Formate Imax und Omnimax, die z.B. in Planetarien verwendet werden.

All diese Eigenschaften werden auf den 100 Leinwanden hier in München repräsentiert werden. Ein genaueres Studium der Filmgeschichte zeigt freilich schnell, daß viele dieser Entwicklungen sich überlappen. So wurden schon früh in der Geschichte des Films Kopien eingefärbt, und mit dem Einfärben des Filmmaterials vor dem Belichten wurde bereits in den 30er Jahren experimentiert. Umgekehrt wurde natürlich nach der Einführung des Farbfilms in vielen Filmen dennoch mit Schwarzweiß gearbeitet, sei es aus ökonomischen oder ästhetischen Gründen. Für Wissenschaftler und vermögende Leute gab es Fernsehen schon vor 1946, und bereits Ende der 20er Jahre hatte Abel Gance Schritte Richtung Breitwand unternommen, indem er durch Zwei- oder Dreifach-Projektion das Bild in die Breite erweiterte.

To complement these five stages, the hundred screens in Munich has been divided into five sequences or 'journeys', all easily and conveniently made on foot.

1. The first sequence is the shortest and a little separated from the others in the north of the city at the Königsplatz. It eulogizes the black and white quality of early 'archaeological' cinema.

2. The second sequence revolves around the Cathedral, Munich's largest religious building and most celebrated landmark.

3. The third sequence makes a large southern loop that takes in the river.

4. The fourth sequence, introducing colour, heralds the Avenue of the Screens along the buildings of the Ludwigstraße, where large flat façades offer ideal screen projection areas.

5. The fifth sequence starts at the Rathaus and spirals ever inwards to the Max-Josephs-Platz. It has the largest number of screen projections, intimating all the technologies of the maturity of cinema from 1946 to the present day.

Diesen fünf Stadien entsprechend sind die 100 Münchner Leinwände in fünf Sequenzen oder Strecken aufgeteilt worden, die sich alle bequem zu Fuß bewältigen lassen.

1. Die erste Sequenz ist die kürzeste und befindet sich etwas abseits der anderen im Norden der Stadt am Königsplatz. Sie preist das Schwarzweiß des frühen »archäologischen« Kinos.

2. Die zweite Sequenz dreht sich um die Frauenkirche, Münchens größten Sakralbau und das berühmteste Wahrzeichen der Stadt.

3. Die dritte Sequenz macht einen großen Bogen Richtung Süden und bezieht den Fluß mit ein.

4. Die vierte Sequenz, die Farbe einführend, verkündet die »Avenue der Leinwände«, entlang der Gebäude der Ludwigstraße, deren breite flachen Fassaden ideale Projektionsflächen darbieten.

5. Die fünfte Sequenz beginnt bei der Staatskanzlei und bewegt sich spiralförmig auf den Max-Josephs-Platz zu, hat am meisten Leinwände und stellt alle technischen Neuerungen von der Reifezeit des Films 1946 bis heute vor.

Details of lighting programme by Reinier van Brummelen

Details des Lichtprogramms von Reinier van Brummelen

1	1895	1	A	100	Staatliche Antikensammlung/ front rechts		distance: ± 45 mtr.
7	1901			94	Staatliche Antikensammlung/ front rechts		
		tower: 8 mtrs			1	1,2 HMI profile 17 Gr.	frames
					2	1,2 HMI profile 9Gr.	years
					3	dimmershutter	
					3	colorscrollers	
					4	par 64 for the tower	
					2	arenavision	
2	1896	2	A	101	Staatliche Antikensammlung/ front links		distance: ± 45 mtr.
8	1902			95	Staatliche Antikensammlung/ front links		
3	1897			98	Propylaen/ front rechts		distance: ± 40 mtr.
4	1903			99	Propylaen/ front rechts		
		tower: 8 mtrs			2	1,2 HMI profile 17 Gr.	frames
					4	1,2 HMI profile 9Gr.	years
					6	dimmershutter	
					6	colorscrollers	
					4	par 64 for the tower	
					4	arenavision	
9	1898	3	A	99b	Propylaen/ front links		distance: ± 40 mtr.
10	1904			99a	Propylaen/ front links		
5	1899			92	Glyptothek / front rechts		distance: ± 45 mtr.
11	1905				Glyptothek / front rechts		
		tower: 8 mtrs			2	1,2 HMI profile 17 Gr.	frames
					4	1,2 HMI profile 9Gr.	years
					6	dimmershutter	
					6	colorscrollers	
					4	par 64 for the tower	
					4	arenavision	
6	1900	4	A	93	Glyptothek / front links		distance: ± 45 mtr.
12	1906				Glyptothek / front links		
		tower: 8 mtrs			1	1,2 HMI profile 17 Gr.	frames
					2	1,2 HMI profile 9Gr.	years
					3	dimmershutter	
					3	colorscrollers	
					4	par 64 for the tower	
					2	arenavision	
13	1907	5	TD1	62	St.Michaelskirche-Ettstr. oberes feld		distance: ± 22 mtr.
14	1908			63	St.Michaelskirche-Ettstr. unteres feld		
		tower: 6 mtrs			4	2k profile 9/32 Gr.	
					4	colorscrollers	
						dimmers	
15	1909	6	NC	23	Polizeistation- Lowengrube/Frauenplatz		distance: ± 25 mtr.
16	1910			23	Polizeistation- Lowengrube/Frauenplatz		distance: ± 20 mtr.
		tower: 6 mtrs			2	1,2 HMI profile 17 Gr.	frames
					2	1,2 HMI profile 9Gr.	years
					4	colorwheel	
17	1911	rf	TD2	20	Freuenkirche- unter linker Turmuhr		distance: ± 75 mtr.
18	1912			22	Freuenkirche- unter rechter Turmuhr		
19	1913				Freuenkirche- unter linker Turmuhr		
20	1914				Freuenkirche- unter rechter Turmuhr		
21	1915				Freuenkirche- mitten		
		roofplatform			10	1,2 HMI profile 9Gr.	years
					10	dimmershutter	
					10	colorscrollers	
					4	arenavision	
22	1916	rf	NC		Alte Peter front		distance: 32 mtr.
		roofplatform			1	1,2 HMI profile 9Gr.	frame
					1	2k profile 9/32 Gr.	year
					2	colorwheel	

23	1917	7	NC	54	Lowenturm/Rosental, Kantenprojection		distance: 40 mtr.
24	1918				Fountain/waterprojection		distance: 12 mtr.
		tower: 6 mtrs			4	2k profile 9/32 Gr.	frames
					3	2k profile 9/32 Gr.	years
					6	colorwheel	
25	1919	8	TD3	49	St. Jacobplatz-links		distance: 37,5 mtr.
26	1920			50	St. Jacobplatz-mitte		distance: 43 mtr.
27	1921			51	St. Jacobplatz-rechts		distance: 38 mtr.
		tower: 8 mtrs			3	1,2 HMI profile 17 Gr.	frame
					3	1,2 HMI profile 9Gr.	years
					6	dimmershutter	
					6	colorscrollers	
28	1922	9	TD3	52	St. Jacobplatz-BP parkhaus links		distance: 45 mtr.
29	1923			53	St. Jacobplatz-BP parkhaus rechts		
		tower: 7 mtrs			2	1,2 HMI profile 17 Gr.	frames
					2	1,2 HMI profile 9Gr.	years
					4	dimmershutter	
					4	colorscrollers	
30	1924	10	NC	48	Munchner Stadtmuseum		distance: 39 mtr.
		tower: 7 mtrs			2	2k profile 9/32 Gr.	frame
					2	2k profile 9/32 Gr.	years
					3	colorwheel	
31	1925	11	NC	45	Wasserturm/Blumenstr. A		distance: 30 mtr.
32	1926				Wasserturm/Blumenstr. A		
		tower: 6 mtrs			2	1,2 HMI profile zoom	frames
					2	1,2 HMI profile 17	years
					4	dimmershutter	
					4	colorscrollers	
33	1927	12	TD4	42	Isator/Im Tal-uber dem tor 1		distance: 31 mtr.
34	1928			43	Isator/Im Tal-uber dem tor 2		
		tower: 8 mtrs			4	2k profile 9/32 Gr.	frame
					2	2k profile 9/32 Gr.	years
					6	dimmershutter	
					6	colorscrollers	
35	1929	rf	TD4	44	Isator-Innenhof		distance: ± 14 mtr.
36	1930				Isator-Innenhof		
		tower: 8 mtrs			4	2k profile 9/32 Gr.	frame
					2	2k profile 9/32 Gr.	years
					6	dimmershutter	
					6	colorscrollers	
37	1931	13	TD5	90	Maximilenium / links von Brunnen		distance: ± 35 mtr.
38	1932	14		91	Maximilenium / rechts von Brunnen		
39	1933			91	Maximilenium / hinten Brunnen		
		2 towers : 4 mtrs			4	1,2 HMI profile 17 Gr.	frames
					3	1,2 HMI profile 17 Gr.	years
					7	dimmershutter	
					7	colorscrollers	
40	1934	15	TD6	65	Haus der Kunst/ Ecke ost		distance: ± 21 mtr.
		tower: 6 mtrs			2	2k profile 9/32 Gr.	frame
					2	2k profile 9/15 Gr.	years
					4	colorscrollers	
						dimmers	
41	1935	16	TD7	65	Haus der Kunst/ Ecke west (haupteingang)		distance: ± 21 mtr.
		tower: 6 mtrs			2	2k profile 9/32 Gr.	frame
					2	2k profile 9/15 Gr.	years
					4	colorscrollers	
						dimmers	

42	1936	17	2	6	Siegestor-front				distance: ± 40 mtr.
		tower:	8 mtrs			2	1,2 HMI profile 17 Gr.	frames	
						1	1,2 HMI profile 9Gr.	years	
						4	colorscrollers		
						3	dimmershutter		
43	1937	18	2		Ludwigstrasse 1				distance: 34,5 mtr.
		tower:	8 mtrs			3	1,2 HMI profile zoom	frames	
						1	2k profile 9/15 Gr.	year	
						4	colorscrollers		
						3	dimmershutter		
						1	dimmer		
44	1938	19	2		Ludwigstrasse 2				distance: 34 mtr.
		tower:	8 mtrs			3	1,2 HMI profile zoom	frame	
						1	2k profile 9/15 Gr.	year	
						4	colorscrollers		
						3	dimmershutter		
						1	dimmer		
45	1939	21	2		Ludwigstrasse 3				distance: 35 mtr.
		tower:	8 mtrs			3	1,2 HMI profile zoom	frame	
						1	2k profile 9/15 Gr.	year	
						4	colorscrollers		
						3	dimmershutter		
						1	dimmer		
46	1940	22	2		Ludwigstrasse 4				distance: 35 mtr.
		tower:	8 mtrs			3	1,2 HMI profile zoom	frame	
						1	2k profile 9/15 Gr.	year	
						4	colorscrollers		
						3	dimmershutter		
						1	dimmer		
47	1941	23	2		Ludwigstrasse 5				distance: 34 mtr.
		tower:	8 mtrs			3	1,2 HMI profile zoom	frame	
						1	2k profile 9/15 Gr.	year	
						4	colorscrollers		
						3	dimmershutter		
						1	dimmer		
48	1942	24	2		Ludwigstrasse 6				distance: 34 mtr.
		tower:	8 mtrs			3	1,2 HMI profile zoom	frame	
						1	2k profile 9/15 Gr.	year	
						4	colorscrollers		
						3	dimmershutter		
						1	dimmer		
49	1943	25	2		Ludwigstrasse 7				distance: 32 mtr.
		tower:	8 mtrs			3	1,2 HMI profile zoom	frame	
						1	2k profile 9/15 Gr.	year	
						4	colorscrollers		
						3	dimmershutter		
						1	dimmer		
50	1944	26	2		Ludwigstrasse 8				distance: 35 mtr.
		tower:	8 mtrs			3	1,2 HMI profile zoom	frame	
						1	2k profile 9/15 Gr.	year	
						4	colorscrollers		
						3	dimmershutter		
						1	dimmer		
51	1945	27	2		Ludwigstrasse 9				distance: 32 mtr.
		tower:	8 mtrs			3	1,2 HMI profile zoom	frame	
						1	2k profile 9/15 Gr.	year	
						4	colorscrollers		
						3	dimmershutter		
						1	dimmer		

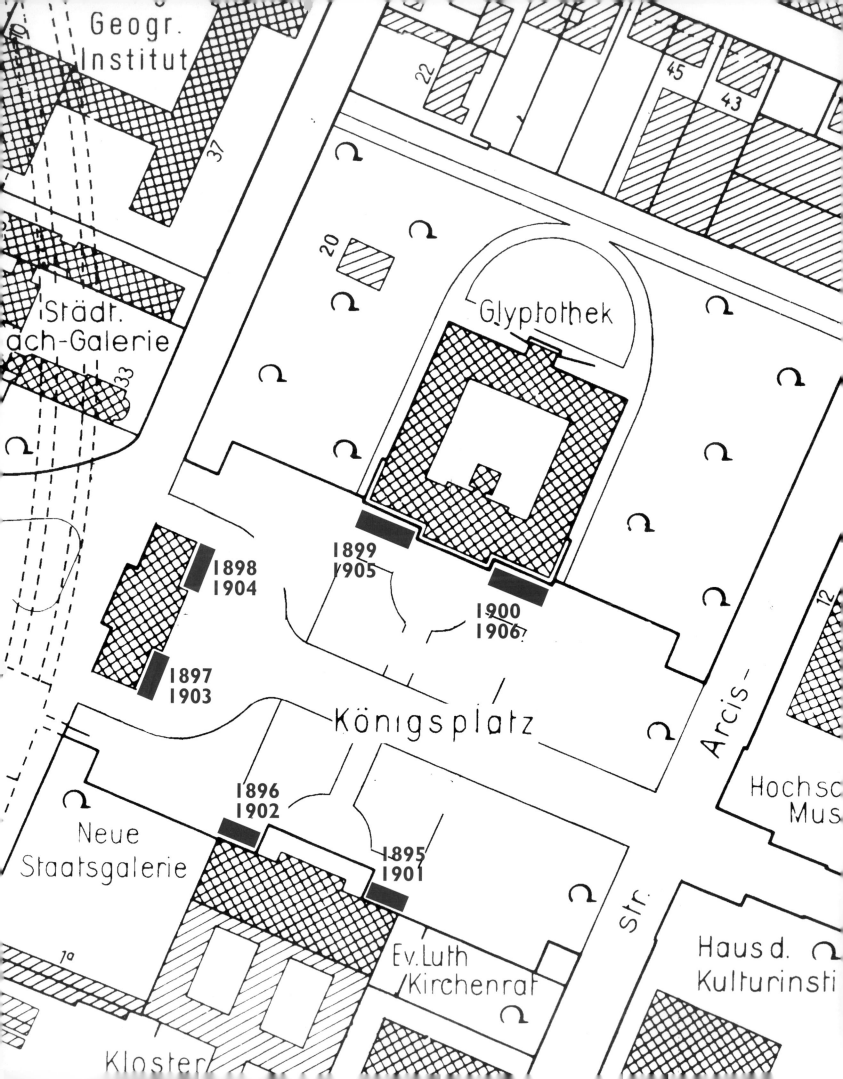

Geogr.
Institut

Städt.
ach-Galerie

Glyptothek

22

45

43

37

20

33

12

1898
1904

1899
1905

1897
1903

1900
1906

Königsplatz

1896
1902

Arcis-

Hochsc
Mus

Neue
Staatsgalerie

1895
1901

7ᵃ

Ev.Luth
/Kirchenrat

Str.

Haus d.
Kulturinsti

Kloster

THE FIRST SEQUENCE

THE KÖNIGSPLATZ SEQUENCE
Years 1895 to 1906
12 screens (double sequence of 6)

Number	Year	Place	Year-Screen Characteristic
1.	1895	Antikensammlung	Black and white
2.	1896	Antikensammlung	Black and white
3.	1897	Propylaeum	Black and white
4.	1898	Propylaeum	Black and white
5.	1899	Glyptothek	Black and white
6.	1900	Glyptothek	Black and white
7.	1901	Antikensammlung	Black and white (tinged blue)
8.	1902	Antikensammlung	Black and white (tinged blue)
9.	1903	Propylaeum	Black and white (tinged green)
10.	1904	Propylaeum	Black and white (tinged red)
11.	1905	Glyptothek	Black and white (tinged red)
12.	1906	Glyptothek	Black and white (tinged green)

ERSTE SEQUENZ

DIE KÖNIGSPLATZ-SEQUENZ
1895–1906
12 Leinwände (Doppel-Sequenz von 6)

Nummer	Jahr	Ort	Eigenschaft
1.	1895	Antikensammlung	schwarzweiß
2.	1896	Antikensammlung	schwarzweiß
3.	1897	Propyläen	schwarzweiß
4.	1898	Propyläen	schwarzweiß
5.	1899	Glyptothek	schwarzweiß
6.	1900	Glyptothek	schwarzweiß
7.	1901	Antikensammlung	schwarzweiß (blau getönt)
8.	1902	Antikensammlung	schwarzweiß (blau getönt)
9.	1903	Propyläen	schwarzweiß (grün getönt)
10.	1904	Propyläen	schwarzweiß (rot getönt)
11.	1905	Glyptothek	schwarzweiß (rot getönt)
12.	1906	Glyptothek	schwarzweiß (grün getönt)

SCREEN 1 **1895**   SCREEN 2 **1896**
SCREEN 7 **1901**   SCREEN 8 **1902**

ANTIKENSAMMLUNG

SCREEN 3 **1897**   SCREEN 4 **1898**
SCREEN 9 **1903**   SCREEN 10 **1904**

PROPYLÄEN

SCREEN 5 **1899**   SCREEN 6 **1900**
SCREEN 11 **1905**   SCREEN 12 **1906**

GLYPTOTHEK

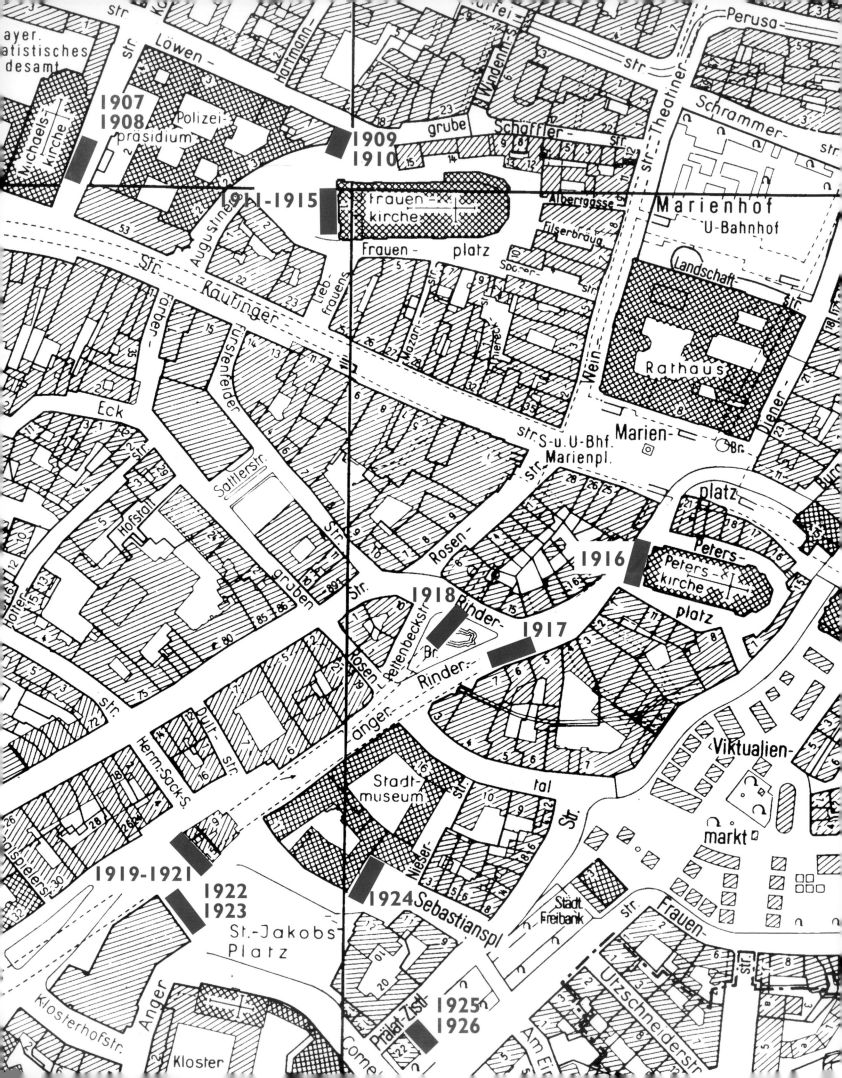

bayer.
atistisches
desamt

**1907
1908**

Michaels-kirche

str

KO

Löwen-

str

Hartmann-

str

Polizei-präsidium

**1909
1910**

1911-1915

28

grube

Schäffer-

str

Theatiner-

str

Perusa-

Schrammer-str

Augustiner-

str

Kaufinger

Lieb-frauen-

Färber-

Frauen-kirche

Frauen-

platz

Albergasse

Filserbräu

Sparer-

str

str

Wein-

str

Marienhof

U-Bahnhof

Landschaft-

str

Rathaus

Eck

Fürstenfelder

Sattlerstr

Hofstatt

str

Rosen-

str

str

str

Str S-u.U-Bhf.
Marien-
Marienpl.

Br.

platz

1916

Peters-

Peters-kirche

platz

gruben

Str

Rosen-

str

1918

Peltenbeckstr

Br.

Rinder-

1917

Rinder-

Anger-

Herm.-Sacks-

Dult-str

Stadt-museum

Niese-str

tal

Str

Viktualien-

markt

1919-1921

**1922
1923**

St.-Jakobs-
Platz

1924 Sebastianspl

Städt.
Freibank

str

Frauen-

Anger

Klosterhofstr

Kloster

Pralat-Zist-

**1925
1926**

Cornelius

Am Ein

Utzschneiderstr

THE SECOND SEQUENCE

THE CATHEDRAL SEQUENCE
Years 1907 to 1926
20 screens

Number	Year	Place	Characteristic
13.	1907	St Michael's Church	Black and white
14.	1908	St Michael's Church	Black and white
15.	1909	Police station	Black and white
16.	1910	Police station	Black and white
17.	1911	Cathedral	Black and white and green
18.	1912	Cathedral	Black and white and red
19.	1913	Cathedral	Black and white and green
20.	1914	Cathedral	Black and white and red
21.	1915	Cathedral	Black and white and orange
22.	1916	Old St Peter's	Black and white
23	1917	Lion Tower	Black and white
24	1918	Bull Fountain	Black and white
25	1919	Sankt-Jakobs-Platz	Black and white
26.	1920	Sankt-Jakobs-Platz	Black and white and blue-green
27.	1921	Sankt-Jakobs-Platz	Black and white
28.	1922	Car-park	Black and white
29.	1923	Car-park	Black and white
30.	1924	Stadtmuseum	Black and white
31.	1925	Bunker	Black and white
32.	1926	Bunker	Black and white

ZWEITE SEQUENZ

DIE FRAUENKIRCHE-SEQUENZ
1907–1926
20 Leinwände

Nummer	Jahr	Ort	Eigenschaft
13.	1907	St. Michael	schwarzweiß
14.	1908	St. Michael	schwarzweiß
15.	1909	Polizeipräsidium	schwarzweiß
16.	1910	Polizeipräsidium	schwarzweiß
17.	1911	Frauenkirche	schwarzweiß und grün
18.	1912	Frauenkirche	schwarzweiß und rot
19.	1913	Frauenkirche	schwarzweiß und grün
20.	1914	Frauenkirche	schwarzweiß und rot
21.	1915	Frauenkirche	schwarzweiß und orange
22.	1916	Alter Peter	schwarzweiß
23.	1917	Löwenturm	schwarzweiß
24.	1918	Rinderbrunnen	schwarzweiß
25.	1919	Sankt-Jakobs-Platz	schwarzweiß
26.	1920	Sankt-Jakobs-Platz	schwarzweiß und blaugrün
27.	1921	Sankt-Jakobs-Platz	schwarzweiß
28.	1922	BP-Parkhaus	schwarzweiß
29.	1923	BP-Parkhaus	schwarzweiß
30.	1924	Stadtmuseum	schwarzweiß
31.	1925	Hochbunker	schwarzweiß
32.	1926	Hochbunker	schwarzweiß

SCREEN 13 **1907**
SCREEN 14 **1908**

ST. MICHAEL

SCREEN 15 **1909**   SCREEN 16 **1910**

POLIZEIPRÄSIDIUM

SCREEN 17 **1911**   SCREEN 19 **1913**

SCREEN 18 **1912**   SCREEN 20 **1914**

SCREEN 21 **1915**

FRAUENKIRCHE

ALTER PETER

LÖWENTURM

SCREEN 24 **1918**

RINDERBRUNNEN

SCREEN 26 **1920**

SCREEN 25 **1919**   SCREEN 27 **1921**

SANKT-JAKOBS-PLATZ

SCREEN 28 **1922**   SCREEN 29 **1923**

BP-PARKHAUS

SCREEN 30 **1924**

STADTMUSEUM

SCREEN 31 **1925**
SCREEN 32 **1926**

HOCHBUNKER

THE THIRD SEQUENCE

THE ISARTORPLATZ TO THE HAUS DER KUNST
Years 1927 to 1935
13 screens

Number	Year	Place	Characteristic
33.	1927	Isartor	Black and white
34.	1928	Isartor	Black and white
35.	1929	Isartor	Black and white
36.	1930	Isartor	Black and white
37.	1931	Maximilianeum	Black and white
38.	1932	Maximilianeum	Black and white
39.	1933	Maximilianeum	Black and white
40.	1934	Haus der Kunst	Black and white
41.	1935	Haus der Kunst	Black and white

DRITTE SEQUENZ

VOM ISARTORPLATZ ZUM HAUS DER KUNST
1927–1935
13 Leinwände

Nummer	Jahr	Ort	Eigenschaft
33.	1927	Isartor	schwarzweiß
34.	1928	Isartor	schwarzweiß
35.	1929	Isartor	schwarzweiß
36.	1930	Isartor	schwarzweiß
37.	1931	Maximilianeum	schwarzweiß
38.	1932	Maximilianeum	schwarzweiß
39.	1933	Maximilianeum	schwarzweiß
40.	1934	Haus der Kunst	schwarzweiß
41.	1935	Haus der Kunst	schwarzweiß

SCREEN 33 **1927**
SCREEN 34 **1928**

ISARTOR

SCREEN 35 **1929**
SCREEN 36 **1930**

ISARTOR

SCREEN 37 **1931**   SCREEN 38 **1932**   SCREEN 39 **1933**

MAXIMILIANEUM

SCREEN 40 **1934**

HAUS DER KUNST

SCREEN 41 **1935**

HAUS DER KUNST

THE FOURTH SEQUENCE

THE LUDWIGSTRASSE: THE AVENUE OF SCREENS
Years 1936 to 1946
11 screens

VIERTE SEQUENZ

DIE LUDWIGSTRASSE: DIE AVENUE DER LEINWÄNDE
1936–1946
11 Leinwände

Number	Year	Place	Characteristic	Nummer	Jahr	Ort	Eigenschaft
42.	1936	Siegestor	Colour	42.	1936	Siegestor	farbig
43.	1937	Prof.-Huber-Platz no. 1	Colour	43.	1937	Professor-Huber-Platz 1	farbig
44.	1938	Ludwigstraße no. 25	Colour	44.	1938	Ludwigstraße 25	farbig
45	1939	Ludwigstraße no. 16	Colour	45.	1939	Ludwigstraße 16	farbig
46	1940	Ludwigstraße no. 16	Colour	46.	1940	Ludwigstraße 16	farbig
47.	1941	Ludwigstraße no. 19	Colour	47.	1942	Ludwigstraße 19	farbig
48.	1942	Ludwigstraße no. 15	Colour	48.	1941	Ludwigstraße 15	farbig
49.	1943	Ludwigstraße no. 10	Colour	49.	1944	Ludwigstraße 10	farbig
50.	1944	Ludwigstraße no. 6	Colour	50.	1943	Ludwigstraße 6	farbig
51.	1945	Ludwigstraße no. 2	Colour	51.	1945	Ludwigstraße 2	farbig

SIEGESTOR

SCREEN 43 **1937**

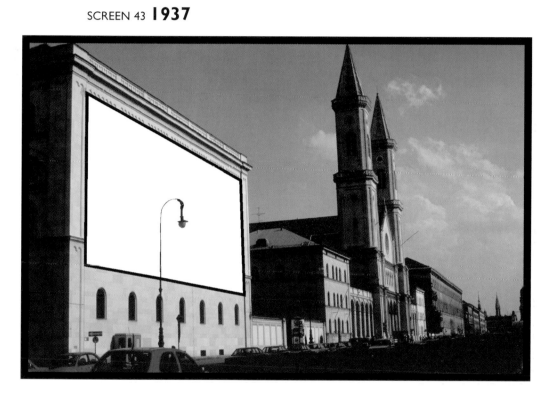

PROFESSOR-HUBER-PLATZ 1

SCREEN 44 **1938**

LUDWIGSTRASSE 25

SCREEN 45 **1939**   SCREEN 46 **1940**

LUDWIGSTRASSE 16

SCREEN 47 **1941**   SCREEN 48 **1942**

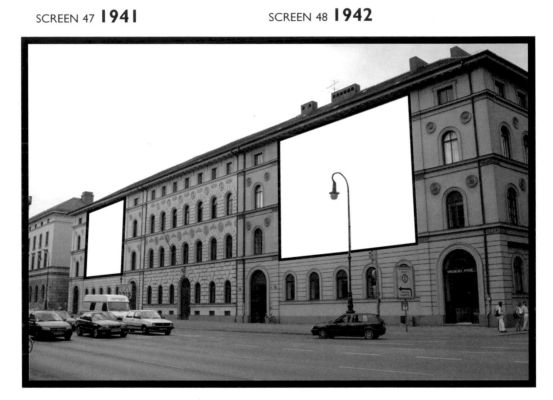

LUDWIGSTRASSE 19 UND 15

SCREEN 49 **1943**   SCREEN 50 **1944**

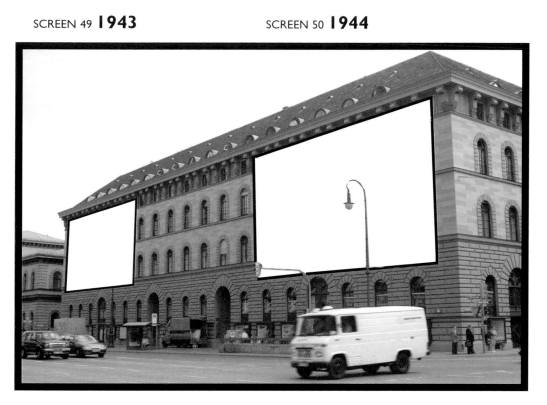

LUDWIGSTRASSE 10 UND 6

SCREEN 51 **1945**

LUDWIGSTRASSE 2

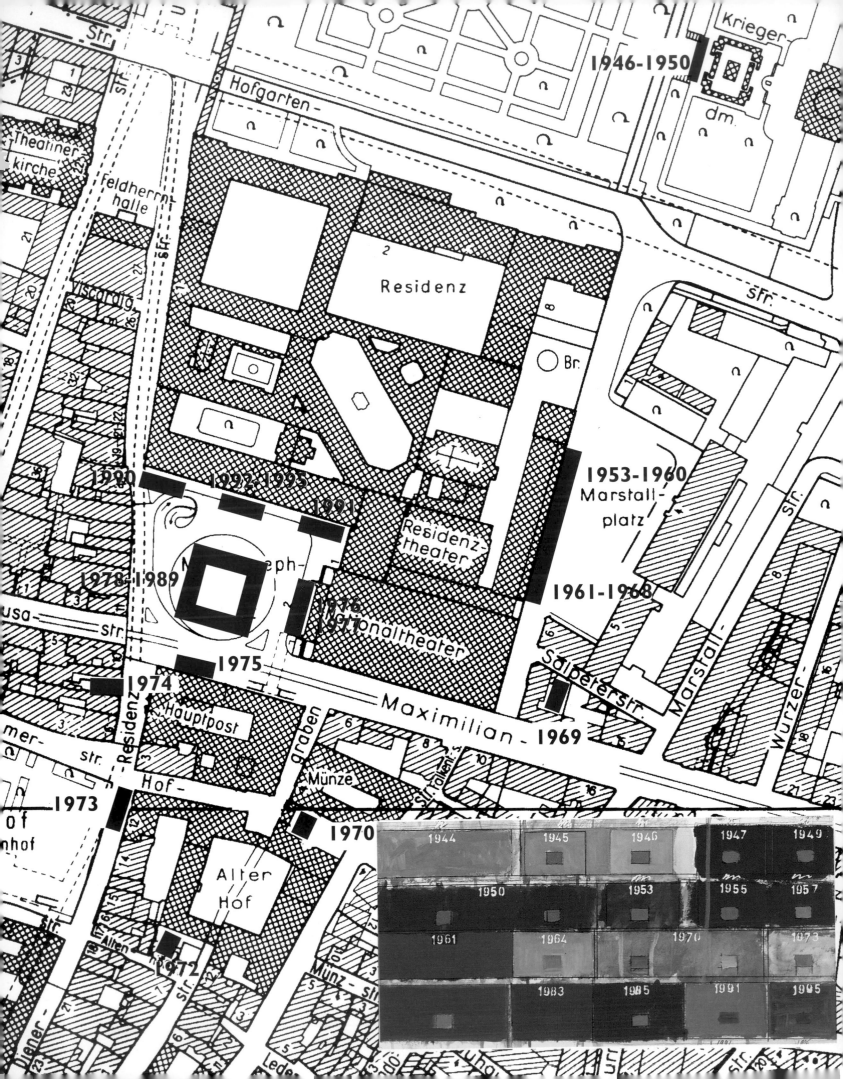

Krieger

1946-1950

dm.

Hofgarten-

Theatiner kirche

Feldherrn halle

str.

Residenz

2

sfr.

Br.

1953-1960
Marstall-
platz

1990   1992-1993
              1991

1978-1989

1961-1968

Nationaltheater

Residenz theater

Salpeterstr.

Marstall-

Wurzer-

str.

1975

1974

Maximilian- 1969

1973

Hauptpost

Münze

1970

Alter
Hof

1972

Münz-   str.

1944	1945	1946	1947	1949
1950	1953	1955	1957
1961	1964	1970	1973
1983	1985	1991	1995

THE FIFTH SEQUENCE

THE MAX-JOSEPH SEQUENCE
Years 1946 to 1995
50 screens

No.	Year	Place	Characteristic
52.	1946	Town Hall	Cinema standard + TV
53.	1947	Town Hall	Cinema standard + TV
54.	1948	Town Hall	Cinema standard + TV
55.	1949	Town Hall	Cinema standard + TV
56.	1950	Town Hall	Cinema standard + TV
57.	1951	Side of Town Hall	Cinema
58.	1952	Side of Town Hall	Cinema
59.	1953	Residenz Theatre	Wide ratio + TV
60.	1954	Residenz Theatre	Wide ratio + TV
61.	1955	Residenz Theatre	Wide ratio + TV
62.	1956	Residenz Theatre	Wide ratio + TV
63.	1957	Residenz Theatre	Wide ratio + TV
64.	1958	Residenz Theatre	Wide ratio + TV
65.	1959	Residenz Theatre	Wide ratio + TV
66.	1960	Residenz Theatre	Wide ratio + TV
67.	1961	Residenz Theatre	Standard ratio + TV
68.	1962	Residenz Theatre	Standard ratio + TV
69.	1963	Residenz Theatre	Standard ratio + TV
70.	1964	Residenz Theatre	Standard ratio + TV
71.	1965	Residenz Theatre	Standard ratio + TV
72.	1966	Residenz Theatre	Standard ratio + TV
73.	1967	Residenz Theatre	Standard ratio + TV
74.	1968	Residenz Theatre	Standard ratio + TV
75.	1969	Maximilianstraße no. 13	Coloured wide screen
76.	1970	Pfisterstraße/Münzbogen	Wide screen
77.	1971	Hofgraben	Wide screen
78.	1972	Altenhofstraße/Burgstraße	Wide screen
79.	1973	Financial building, Marienhof	Wide screen
80.	1974	Residenzstraße no. 7	Wide screen
81.	1975	Törringpalais	Wide screen
82.	1976	National Theatre gable	Colour TV
83.	1977	National Theatre gable	Colour TV
84.	1978	Paving stones of Max-Josephs-Platz	Standard ratio
85.	1979	Paving stones of Max-Josephs-Platz	Standard ratio
86.	1980	Paving stones of Max-Josephs-Platz	Standard ratio
87.	1981	Paving stones of Max-Josephs-Platz	Standard ratio
88.	1982	Paving stones of Max-Josephs-Platz	Standard ratio
89.	1983	Paving stones of Max-Josephs-Platz	Standard ratio
90.	1984	Paving stones of Max-Josephs-Platz	Standard ratio
91.	1985	Paving stones of Max-Josephs-Platz	Standard ratio
92.	1986	Paving stones of Max-Josephs-Platz	Standard ratio
93.	1987	Paving stones of Max-Josephs-Platz	Standard ratio
94.	1988	Paving stones of Max-Josephs-Platz	Standard ratio
95.	1989	Paving stones of Max-Josephs-Platz	Standard ratio
96	1990	Residenz	Imax
97	1991	Residenz	Imax
98	1992	Residenz	Omnimax
99	1993	Residenz	Omnimax
100	1994	Residenz	Omnimax
101	1995	Residenz	Omnimax

FÜNFTE SEQUENZ

DIE MAX-JOSEPH-SEQUENZ
1946–1995
50 Leinwände

Nr	Jahr	Ort	Eigenschaft	
52.	1946	Staatskanzlei	Kino-Standardformat + TV	
53.	1947	Staatskanzlei	Kino-Standardformat + TV	
54.	1948	Staatskanzlei	Kino-Standardformat + TV	
55.	1949	Staatskanzlei	Kino-Standardformat + TV	
56.	1950	Staatskanzlei	Kino-Standardformat + TV	
57.	1951	Staatskanzlei/Südseite	Kino	
58.	1952	Staatskanzlei/Südseite	Kino	
59.	1953	Residenztheater	Breitwand + TV	
60.	1954	Residenztheater	Breitwand + TV	
61.	1955	Residenztheater	Breitwand + TV	
62.	1956	Residenztheater	Breitwand + TV	
63.	1957	Residenztheater	Breitwand + TV	
64.	1958	Residenztheater	Breitwand + TV	
65.	1959	Residenztheater	Breitwand + TV	
66.	1960	Residenztheater	Breitwand + TV	
67.	1961	Residenztheater	Standardformat + TV	
68.	1962	Residenztheater	Standardformat + TV	
69.	1963	Residenztheater	Standardformat + TV	
70.	1964	Residenztheater	Standardformat + TV	
71.	1965	Residenztheater	Standardformat + TV	
72.	1966	Residenztheater	Standardformat + TV	
73.	1967	Residenztheater	Standardformat + TV	
74.	1968	Residenztheater	Standardformat + TV	
75.	1969	Maximilianstraße 13	Breitwand	farbig
76.	1970	Pfisterstraße/Münzbogen	Breitwand	
77.	1971	Hofgraben	Breitwand	
78.	1972	Altenhofstraße/Burgstraße	Breitwand	
79.	1973	Finanzamt Marienhof	Breitwand	
80.	1974	Residenzstraße 7	Breitwand	
81.	1975	Törringpalais	Breitwand	
82.	1976	Operngiebel	TV farbig	
83.	1977	Operngiebel	TV farbig	
84.	1978	Pflastersteine Max-Josephs-Platz	Standard	
85.	1979	Pflastersteine Max-Josephs-Platz	Standard	
86.	1980	Pflastersteine Max-Josephs-Platz	Standard	
87.	1981	Pflastersteine Max-Josephs-Platz	Standard	
88.	1982	Pflastersteine Max-Josephs-Platz	Standard	
89.	1983	Pflastersteine Max-Josephs-Platz	Standard	
90.	1984	Pflastersteine Max-Josephs-Platz	Standard	
91.	1985	Pflastersteine Max-Josephs-Platz	Standard	
92.	1986	Pflastersteine Max-Josephs-Platz	Standard	
93.	1987	Pflastersteine Max-Josephs-Platz	Standard	
94.	1988	Pflastersteine Max-Josephs-Platz	Standard	
95.	1989	Pflastersteine Max-Josephs-Platz	Standard	
96.	1990	Residenz	Imax	
97.	1991	Residenz	Imax	
98.	1992	Residenz	Omnimax	
99.	1993	Residenz	Omnimax	
100.	1994	Residenz	Omnimax	
101.	1995	Residenz	Omnimax	

STAATSKANZLEI

SCREEN 57 **1951**
SCREEN 58 **1952**

STAATSKANZLEI

SCREENS 59-66 **1953-1960**
SCREENS 67-74 **1961-1968**

RESIDENZTHEATER/MARSTALLPLATZ

SCREEN 7,5 **1969**

MAXIMILIANSTRASSE 13

SCREEN 76 **1970**

RESIDENZTHEATER/MARSTALLPLATZ

SCREEN 77 **1971**

HOFGRABEN

SCREEN 78 **1972**

ALTENHOFSTRASSE/BURGSTRASSE

SCREEN 79 **1973**

FINANZAMT MARIENHOF

SCREEN 80 **1974**

RESIDENZSTRASSE 7

SCREEN 81 **1975**

TÖRRINGPALAIS

SCREEN 82 **1976**

SCREEN 83 **1977**

OPERNGIEBEL

PFLASTERSTEINE MAX-JOSEPHS-PLATZ

SCREEN 96 **1990** SCREENS 98-101 **1992-1995** SCREEN 97 **1991**

RESIDENZ

THE STAIRS MUNICH PART TWO

THE STAIRS MÜNCHEN TEIL ZWEI

This second part of THE STAIRS catalogue for the 1995 Munich exhibition is a photographic record of the one hundred light projection screens that have been selected to represent one hundred years of cinema. To appreciate the multiplicity of projections and the possibility of viewing several of them at one time in their architectural context, many of the photographs contain more than one screen.

The one hundred projections in Munich are deliberately non-figurative, since this city installation specifically refers to the essential act of light projection which is the basic premise of cinema. Considering the millions of films manufactured in the last hundred years and the multiplicity of uses to which film has been put, it could be said that the disciplined projection of light is the only true common factor. But, as if to remind us in the briefest possible way of the uses to which this act of projection has been put, the catalogue also contains a list of one thousand films running as a continuous frieze under the photographs of the Munich projection sites, with ten films being selected for each year of the century. Although there are of course a great many films to choose from, the criterion for inclusion is not necesssarily my subjective appreciation, but the presentation of a cross-section, and perhaps to indicate the various ways in which cinema has proselytized and advertised itself in popular, commercial, aesthetic, political and social terms.

I take this opportunity to thank and applaud all those many people – curators, sponsors, benefactors, administrators, designers, researchers, electricians and many, many others – who have collaborated on this project, and I am sure they would not mind me singling out just two names to represent the large effort necessary to make this project a success: Reinier van Brummelen, who is responsible for the planning and execution of the ambitious lighting plan and whose inexhaustible attention to the whole scheme and its many details is, as always, exemplary, and Elisabeth Schweeger, without whose enthusiasm and consistent support this project would not have been conceived at all in Munich.

Peter Greenaway

Der zweite Teil des Kataloges THE STAIRS über die Ausstellung in München ist eine photographische Erinnerung an 100 Lichtprojektionswände, die ausgewählt wurden, um 100 Jahre Kino zu repräsentieren. Um die Vielzahl der Projektionen schätzen zu können und die Möglichkeit, mehrere auf einmal in ihrem architektonischen Kontext zu sehen, zeigen viele Photographien mehr als nur eine Leinwand.

Die 100 Projektionen in München sind absichtlich nicht-figurativ, denn diese Stadtinstallation bezieht sich in spezifischer Weise auf den essentiellen Akt der Lichtprojektion – der Grundvoraussetzung für Kino. Wenn man an die Millionen von Filmen denkt, die in den letzten 100 Jahren hergestellt worden sind und an die unendlich vielen Verwendungszwecke, für die der Film herhalten mußte, könnte man sagen, daß die disziplinierte Projektion von Licht der einzig wahre gemeinsame Faktor ist. Aber, um uns in komprimiertester Weise an die vielen Arten der Verwendung des Films zu erinnern, enthält der Katalog auch eine Liste von 1000 Filmen, die wie ein fortgesetztes Fries unter den Photos der Münchner Projektionsorte laufen, – 10 Filme für jedes Jahr des Jahrhunderts. Obwohl die Auswahl aus einer Unmenge von Filmen getroffen wurde, sind die Kriterien der gegenwärtigen Einbeziehung nicht unbedingt die meiner persönlichen Vorlieben, aber es ist ein Querschnitt, der vielleicht die unterschiedlichen Wege anzeigt, mit denen das Kino Anhänger gewonnen hat und sich selbst in populärer, kommerzieller, ästhischer, politischer und sozialer Hinsicht beworben hat.

Ich möchte die Gelegenheit nützen, um all den vielen Menschen – Kuratoren, Sponsoren, Unterstützern, Administratoren, Designern, wissenschaftlichen Mitarbeitern, Lichttechnikern und vielen, vielen anderen, die an diesem Projekt mitgearbeitet haben – zu danken, und ich bin sicher, daß sie nichts dagegen haben, wenn ich an dieser Stelle zwei Namen heraushebe, die für den großen Aufwand stehen, der notwendig war, um dieses Projekt erfolgreich werden zu lassen – Reinier van Brummelen, der verantwortlich war für die Planung und Ausführung des ambitiösen Lichtkonzeptes und dessen unerschöpfliche Aufmerksamkeit für die Sache im Ganzen und im Detail exemplarisch war, und Elisabeth Schweeger, ohne deren Enthusiasmus und ständiger Unterstützung dieses Projekt in München nicht vorstellbar gewesen wäre.

Peter Greenaway

1895

La Sortie des usines
France *Auguste/Louis Lumière*
La Peche aux poissons rouges
France *Auguste/Louis Lumière*
Le Jardinier
France *Auguste/Louis Lumière*
La Mer
France *Auguste/Louis Lumière*
L'Arrivee du Train en gare
France *Auguste/Louis Lumière*
L'Arroseur arrosé
France *Auguste/Louis Lumière*
The Derby
Britain *Birt Acres*
Rough Sea at Dover
Britain *Birt Acres*
The Execution of Mary Queen of Scots
USA *Alfred Clark/Thomas Edison*
Griffo v. Barnett Fight
USA *Latham Brothers*

1896

La Biche au bois
France *Georges Demeny*
Escamotage d'une dame chez
Robert Houdin
France *Georges Méliès*
Le Manoir du Diable
France *Georges Méliès*
The Broken Melody
Britain *Esme Collings*
Comic Faces
Britain *G. A. Smith*
The Maid in the Garden
Britain *G. A. Smith*
Persimmon Wins the Derby
Britain *R. W. Paul*
The Soldier's Courtship
Britain *R W Paul*
The Bullfight
USA *Latham/E Louis*
The Irwin-Rice Kiss
USA *Thomas Edison*

1897	1898
L'Auberge ensorcelée France *Georges Méliès*	**La Damnation de Faust** France *Georges Méliès*
Le Cabinet de Méphistophélès France *Georges Méliès*	**Faust et Marguerite** France *Georges Méliès*
Les Dernières Cartouches France *Georges Méliès*	**Un Homme de têtes** France *Georges Méliès*
The Haunted Castle Britain *G.A. Smith*	**Panorama pris d'un ballon captif** France *Georges Méliès*
Making Sausages Britain *G.A. Smith*	**Panorama pris d'un train en marche** France *Georges Méliès*
The Miller and the Sweep Britain *G.A. Smith*	**La Tentation de Saint Antoine** France *Georges Méliès*
Weary Willie Britain *G.A. Smith*	**Cinderella and the Fairy Godmother** Britain *G.A. Smith*
Queen Victoria's Diamond Jubilee Britain	**The Clown Barber** Britain *James Williamson*
The Corbett-Fitzsimmons Fight USA	**Two Naughty Boys** Britain *James Williamson*
The Horitz Passion Play USA *Klaw/Erlanger*	**The Passion Play of Oberammergau** USA *Richard Hollaman*

1899

L'Affaire Dreyfus
France *Georges Méliès*
Cendrillon
France *Georges Méliès*
L'Homme protéé
France *Georges Méliès*
Lightning Robber Being Arrested
Japan *Shiro Asano*
The Bombardment of Mafeking
Britain *Robert Ashe/R.W. Paul*
The Kiss in the Tunnel
Britain *G.A. Smith*
Thrilling Fight on a Scaffold
Britain *R.W. Paul*
Shooting a Boer Spy
Britain *Robert Ashe/R.W. Paul*
The Jeffries-Sharkey Fight
USA
The Tramp's Dream
USA *Sigmund Lubin*

1900

L'Homme-orchestre
France *Georges Méliès*
Jeanne d'Arc
France *Georges Méliès*
Rêve de Noël
France *Georges Méliès*
Attack on a Chinese Mission
Britain *James Williamson*
The Explosion of a Motor-Car
Britain *Cecil Hepworth*
Grandma's Reading Glass
Britain *G.A. Smith*
The Last Days of Pompeii
Britain *R.W. Paul*
La Fée aux choux
Australia *Alice Guy*
Soldiers of the Cross
Australia *Joseph Parry*
Chinese Massacring Christians
USA *Sigmund Lubin*

1901

A la Conquête de l'air
France *Ferdinand Zecca/Pathé*
L'Histoire d'un crime
France *Ferdinand Zecca/Pathé*
Le Petit Chaperon rouge
France *Georges Méliès*
Barbe-Bleue
France *Georges Méliès*
Are You There?
Britain *James Williamson*
The Big Swallow
Britain *James Williamson*
The Magic Sword
Britain *W.R. Booth/R.W. Paul*
Scrooge
Britain *W.R. Booth/R.W. Paul*
The Execution of Czolgosz
USA *Edwin S. Porter*
Jack and the Beanstalk
USA *Edwin S. Porter*

1902

L'Armoire des Frères Davenport
France *Georges Méliès*
La Catastrophe du ballon 'Pax'
France *Georges Méliès*
Robinson Crusoe
France *Georges Méliès*
Les Voyages de Gulliver
France *Georges Méliès*
Le Voyage dans la lune
France *Georges Méliès*
Les Victimes de l'alcoolisme
France *Ferdinand Zecca*
Eruption volcanique à la Martinique
France *Georges Méliès*
The Coronation of King Edward VII
Britain *George Méliès/G.A. Smith/Warwick*
Peace with Honour
Britain *Cecil Hepworth*
Appointment by Telephone
USA *Edwin S. Porter*

1903

La Belle au bois dormant
France *Pathé*
Don Quichotte
France *Pathé*
La Lanterne magique
France *Georges Méliès*
Alice in Wonderland
Britain *Cecil Hepworth/Percy Stow*
**Mary Jane's Mishap, or Don't Fool with
the Paraffin**
Britain *G.A. Smith*
The Great City Fire
Britain *Warwick*
**Weary Willie and Tired Tim – The
Gunpowder Plot**
Britain *Warwick*
East Lynne
USA *Vitagraph*
The Great Train Robbery
USA *Edwin S. Porter/Edison*
Uncle Tom's Cabin
USA *Edwin S. Porter/Edison*

1904

La Bonne purge
France *Pathé*
Indiens et cowboys
France *Pathé*
La Damnation du Dr Faust
France *Georges Méliès*
Le Merveilleux Eventail vivant
France *Georges Méliès*
Le Voyage à travers l'impossible
France *Georges Méliès*
Attack on a Russian Outpost
Britain *Gaumont*
The Sign of the Cross
Britain *Walter Haggar*
The Moonshiners
USA *Biograph*
The Suburbanite
USA *Biograph*
Tom, Tom, the Piper's Son
USA *Biograph*

1905

L'Ange de Noël
France *Georges Méliès*
Les Invisibles
France *Gaston Velle*
Le Palais des mille et une nuits
France *Georges Méliès*
**Le Raid Paris-Monte Carlo en deux
heures**
France *Georges Méliès*
La Révolution en Russie
France *Lucien Nonguet/Pathé*
La presa di Roma
Italia *Filoteo Alberini*
El hotel eléctrico
España *Segundo de Chomón*
Rescued by Rover
Britain *Lewin Fitzhamon/Cecil Hepworth*
The Miller's Daughter
USA *Edwin S. Porter/McCutcheon*
Raffles the Amateur Cracksman
USA *Vitagraph*

1906

Der Hauptmann von Köpenick
Deutschland *H.B. Baeckers*
C'est Papa qui prend la purge
France *Louis Feuillade*
Le Poison
France *Louis Gasnier*
Les Quatre Cent Farces du Diable
France *George Méliès*
Nozze tragiche
Italia *Gaston Velle*
The Saucy Magazine
Britain *Gaumont*
The Curate's Dilemma
Britain *R.W. Paul*
The Story of the Kelly Gang
Australia *Charles Tait*
Dick Turpin's Ride to New York
USA *Lewin Fitzhamon/Cecil Hepworth*
Automobile Thieves
USA *Vitagraph*

1907	1908
Les Débuts d'un patineur	**L'Assassinat du duc de Guise**
France *Louis Gasnier*	France *Charles Le Bargy/André Calmettes*
L'Enfant prodigue	**La Civilisation à travers les âges**
France *Michel Carré*	France *Georges Méliès*
Hamlet, Prince de Danemark	**Fantasmagorie**
France *Georges Méliès*	France *Emile Cohl*
Le Petit Jules Verne	**Calino Toreador**
France Gaston Velle	Italia *Aquila*
Le avventure di Pulcinella	**In the Land of Nod**
Italy *Gaston Velle*	Britain *Arthur Melbourne-Cooper*
The Boy, the Bust and the Bath	**His First Visit to Warsaw**
USA *Vitagraph*	Poland *Antoni Fertner*
Jack the Kisser	**The Diligent Batman**
USA *Edwin S. Porter*	Rußland *N. Filipov/Drankov*
Rescued from an Eagle's Nest	**The Adventures of Dollie**
USA *J. Searle Dawley/Edison*	USA *D.W. Griffith/AB*
The Teddy Bears	**Bronco Billy and the Baby**
USA *Edwin S. Porter*	USA *G.M. Anderson*
When We Were Boys	**The Fatal Hour**
USA *William N. Selig*	USA *D.W. Griffith/AB*

1909	1910
Mutterliebe	**Aux Lions les Chrétiens**
Deutschland *Duskes*	France *Louis Feuillade*
Le Dernier Requiem de Mozart	**Les Deux Orphelines**
France *E. Arnaud/Gaumont*	France *Albert Capellani*
Giulio Cesare	**The Idiot**
Italia *Giovanni Pastrone*	Rußland *Pyotr Chardynin*
Nerone	**The Pedlars**
Italia *Luigi Maggi/Arturo Ambrosio*	Rußland *Vasili Goncharov*
Otello	**The Queen of Spades**
Italia *Gerolamo Lo Savio*	Rußland *Pyotr Chardynin*
Salomé Mad	**An Arcadian Maid**
Britain *Theo Bouwmeister/Cecil Hepworth*	USA *D.W. Griffith*
Madame Sans-Gêne	**A Child of the Ghetto**
Dänemark *Viggo Larsen*	USA *D.W. Griffith*
The Curtain Pole	**In Old California**
USA *Mack Sennett/AB*	USA *D.W. Griffith*
The Life of George Washington	**Ramona**
USA *Vitagraph*	USA *D.W. Griffith*
A Midsummer Night's Dream	**A Romance of the Western Hills**
USA *Vitagraph*	USA *D.W. Griffith*

1911

La Dame aux Camélias
France *André Calmettes*
Les Hallucinations du Baron Münchhausen
France *Georges Méliès*
Les Misérables
France *Albert Capellani*
Les Mystères de Paris
France *Albert Capellani*
Les Vipères
France *Louis Feuillade*
Henry VIII
Britain *Will Barker*
Richard III
Britain *Frank Benson*
Quo Vadis, Spiridon?
Griechenland *Spiros Dimitrakopoulos*
The Tale of the Fisherman and the Little Fish
Rußland *Kai Henson*
The Lonedale Operator
USA *D.W. Griffith*

1912

La Reine Elisabeth
France *Louis Mercanton*
Cendrillon
France *Georges Méliès*
Oliver Twist
Britain *Thomas Bentley*
Anny – Story of a Prostitute
Norwegen *Adam Eriksen*
The Great Man goes for a Walk
Rußland *Yakov Protazanov/Elizaveta Thiemann*
From the Manger to the Cross
USA *Sidney Olcott*
The Massacre
USA *D.W. Griffith*
The Musketeers of Pig Alley
USA *D.W. Griffith*
The New York Hat
USA *D.W. Griffith*
The Prisoner of Zenda
USA *Edwin S. Porter*

1913

L'Agonie de Byzance
France *Louis Feuillade*
Germinal
France *Albert Capellani*
Quo Vadis?
Italia *Enrico Guazzoni*
East Lynne
Britain *Bert Haldane*
The Pickwick Papers
Britain *Larry Trimble*
The Bartered Bride
Tschechoslowake *Max Urban*
The Grasshopper and the Ant
Rußland *Ladislas Starevich*
The Twilight of a Woman's Soul
Rußland *Evgeni Bauer*
The Loyal Forty-Seven Ronin
Japan *Shozo Makino*
The Squaw Man
USA *Cecil B. De Mille*

1914

Der Golem
Deutschland *Paul Wegener/Henrik Galeen*
Cabiria
Italia *Giovanni Pastrone*
The Girl from Marsh Croft
Schweden *Victor Sjöström*
Anna Karenina
Rußland *Vladimir Gardin*
Katusha
Japan *Kiyumatsu Hosoyama*
Dough and Dynamite
USA *Charlie Chaplin*
Gertie the Dinosaur
USA *Winsor McCay*
The Perils of Pauline
USA *Louis Gasnier*
Tillie's Punctured Romance
USA *Mack Sennett*
The Virginian
USA *Cecil B. De Mille*

1915

Die Unteroffiziere
Deutschland *Alfred Halm*
La Folie du Dr Tube
France *Abel Gance*
Sweet Lavender
Britain *Cecil Hepworth*
Fun at Finglas Fair
Eire *F.J. McCormick*
The Picture of Dorian Gray
Rußland *Vsevelod Emilievich Meyerhold*
War and Peace
Rußland *Vladimir Gardin*
The Birth of a Nation
USA *D.W. Griffith*
The Cheat
USA *Cecil B. De Mille*
Carmen
USA *Cecil B. De Mille*
The Champion
USA *Charlie Chaplin*

1916

Homunculus
Deutschland *Otto Rampert*
Das Tagebuch des Dr. Hart
Deutschland *Paul Leni*
Judex
France *Louis Feuillade*
The Battle of the Somme
Britain *Geoffrey Malins/J. B. McDowell*
A Life for a Life
Rußland *Evgeni Bauer*
The Queen of Spades
Rußland *Yakov Protazanov*
The Count
USA *Charlie Chaplin*
The Floorwalker
USA *Charlie Chaplin*
The Pawnshop
USA *Charlie Chaplin*
Intolerance
USA *D.W. Griffith*

1917

Lulu
Deutschland *Alexander von Antalffy*
Mater Dolorosa
France *Abel Gance*
Masks and Faces
Britain *Fred Paul*
Harrison and Barrison
Ungarn *Sandor Korda*
The Living Corpse
Japan *Ikeru Shikabane*
The Cure
USA *Charlie Chaplin*
Easy Street
USA *Charlie Chaplin*
Rebecca of Sunnybrook Farm
USA *Marshal Neilan*
The Tornado
USA *John Ford*
The Woman God Forgot
USA *Cecil B. De Mille*

1918

Carmen
Deutschland *Ernst Lubitsch*
Die Spinnen
Deutschland *Fritz Lang*
J'Accuse
France *Abel Gance*
Tih Minh
France *Louis Feuillade*
The Outlaw and his Wife
Schweden *Victor Sjöström*
The Lady and the Hooligan
UdSSR *Vladimir Mayakovski*
Blind Husbands
USA *Erich von Stroheim*
A Dog's Life
USA *Charlie Chaplin*
Don't Change Your Husband
USA *Cecil B. De Mille*
Hearts of the World
USA *D.W. Griffith*

1919

Das Kabinett des Dr. Caligari
Deutschland *Robert Wiene*
Der Knabe in Blau
Deutschland *F.W. Murnau*
Madame Dubarry
Deutschland *Ernst Lubitsch*
La Fête espagnole
France *Germaine Dulac*
Leaves from Satan's Book
Dänemark *Carl Theodor Dreyer*
Herr Arne's Treasure
Schweden *Mauritz Stiller*
The Sons of Ingmar
Schweden *Victor Sjöström*
The White Rose
Ungarn *Sandor Korda*
Broken Blossoms
USA *D.W. Griffith*
Why Change Your Wife?
USA *Cecil B. De Mille*

1920

Anna Boleyn
Deutschland *Ernst Lubitsch*
Alf's Button
Britain *Cecil Hepworth*
Wuthering Heights
Britain *A.V. Bramble*
The Parson's Widow
Dänemark *Carl Theodor Dreyer*
Erotikon
Schweden *Mautritz Stiller*
Karen Ingmarsdotter
Schweden *Victor Sjöström*
The Butterfly Man
USA *Ida May Park*
Dr. Jekyll and Mr. Hyde
USA *John S. Robertson*
The Mark of Zorro
USA *Fred Niblo*
Way Down East
USA *D.W. Griffith*

1921

Die Bergkatze
Deutschland *Ernst Lubitsch*
Der müde Tod
Deutschland *Fritz Lang*
L'Atlantide
France *Jacques Feyder*
La Roue
France *Abel Gance*
The Hound of the Baskervilles
Britain *Maurice Elvey*
Thy Soul Shall Bear Witness
Schweden *Victor Sjöström*
Dream Street
USA *D.W. Griffith*
The Kid
USA *Charlie Chaplin*
The Prisoner of Zenda
USA *Rex Ingram*
The Three Musketeers
USA *Fred Niblo*

1922

Der brennende Acker
Deutschland *F.W. Murnau*
Dr. Mabuse der Spieler
Deutschland *Fritz Lang*
**Nosferatu, eine Symphonie des
Grauens**
Deutschland *F.W. Murnau*
Sodom und Gomorrah
Österreich *Michael Curtiz*
Cirano di Bergerac
Italia *Augusto Genina*
Witchcraft through the Ages
Schweden *Benjamin Christensen*
When Love Returns
Japan *Kenji Mizoguchi*
Orphans of the Storm
USA *D.W. Griffith*
Nanook of the North
USA *Robert J. Flaherty*
Cops
USA *Buster Keaton*

1923

Der Schatz
Deutschland *Georg Wilhelm Pabst*
Siegfried
Deutschland *Fritz Lang*
Ménilmontant
France *Dimitri Kirsanoff*
Paris qui dort
France *René Clair*
Le Retour à la raison
France *Man Ray*
Comin' Thro' the Rye
Britain *Cecil Hepworth*
Gösta Berling's Saga
Schweden *Mauritz Stiller*
Greed
USA *Erich von Stroheim*
The Ten Commandments
USA *Cecil B. De Mille*
A Woman of Paris
USA *Charlie Chaplin*

1924

Der letzte Mann
Deutschland *F.W. Murnau*
Michael
Deutschland *Carl Theodor Dreyer*
Kriemhilds Rache
Deutschland *Fritz Lang*
Das Wachsfigurenkabinett
Deutschland *Paul Leni*
Entr'acte
France *René Clair*
Ballet mécanique
France *Fernand Léger*
Smouldering Fires
USA *Clarence Brown*
The Thief of Baghdad
USA *Raoul Walsh*
The Navigator
USA *Buster Keaton*
The Three Ages
USA *Buster Keaton*

1925

Tartüff
Deutschland *F.W. Murnau*
Metropolis
Deutschland *Fritz Lang*
The Pleasure Garden
Britain *Alfred Hitchcock*
Master of the House
Dänemark *Carl Theodor Dreyer*
Battleship Potemkin
UdSSR *Sergei Eisenstein*
The Gold Rush
USA *Charlie Chaplin*
Lady Windermere's Fan
USA *Ernst Lubitsch*
Seven Chances
USA *Buster Keaton*
The Lost World
USA *Harry O. Hoyt*
The Merry Widow
USA *Erich von Stroheim*

1926

Der Student von Prag
Deutschland *Henrik Galeen*
Napoléon
France *Abel Gance*
Nana
France *Jean Renoir*
Stride, Soviet!
UdSSR *Dziga Vertov*
Mother
UdSSR *Vsevolod Pudovkin*
The Strong Man
USA *Frank Capra*
What Price Glory?
USA *Raoul Walsh*
The Big Parade
USA *King Vidor*
Ben Hur
USA *Fred Niblo*
Beau Geste
USA *Herbert Brenon*

1927

Berlin, Symphonie einer Großstadt
Deutschland *Walter Ruttmann*
Un Chapeau de paille d'Italie
France *René Clair*
The End of St Petersburg
UdSSR *Vsevolod Pudovkin*
Sunrise
USA *F.W. Murnau*
The Jazz Singer
USA *Alan Crosland*
The King of Kings
USA *Cecil B. De Mille*
The Underworld
USA *Josef von Sternberg*
The Wedding March
USA *Erich von Stroheim*
The General
USA *Buster Keaton*
Long Pants
USA *Frank Capra*

1928

Spione
Deutschland *Fritz Lang*
Die Büchse von Pandora
Deutschland *Georg Wilhelm Pabst*
La Passion de Jeanne d'Arc
France *Carl Theodor Dreyer*
Un Chien Andalou
France *Luis Buñuel*
La Coquille et le clergyman
France *Germaine Dulac*
Blackmail
Britain *Alfred Hitchcock*
October
UdSSR *Sergei Eisenstein*
The Air Circus
USA *Howard Hawks*
The Crowd
USA *King Vidor*
The Patriot
USA *Ernst Lubitsch*

1929

Regen
Nederlands *Joris Ivens*
Drifters
Britain *John Grierson*
Blackmail
Schweden *Alfred Hitchcock*
The General Line
UdSSR *Sergei Eisenstein*
Man with a Movie-Camera
UdSSR *Dziga Vertov*
I Graduated But . . .
Japan *Yasujiro Ozu*
Applause
USA *Rouben Mamoulian*
The Gold Diggers of Broadway
USA *Roy Del Ruth*
Noah's Ark
USA *Michael Curtiz*
The Skeleton Dance
USA *Walt Disney*

1930

Der blaue Engel
Deutschland *Josef von Sternberg*
Sous les toîts de Paris
France *René Clair*
L'Âge d'Or
France *Luis Buñuel*
Le Sang d'un poète
France *Jean Cocteau*
The Informer
Britain *Arthur Robison*
Earth
UdSSR *Alexander Dovzhenko*
All Quiet on the Western Front
USA *Lewis Milestone*
Animal Crackers
USA *Victor Heerman*
Little Caesar
USA *Mervyn LeRoy*
The Virginian
USA *Victor Fleming*

1931

Kameradschaft
Deutschland *Georg Wilhelm Pabst*
Die Dreigroschenoper
Deutschland *Georg Wilhelm Pabst*
M
Deutschland *Fritz Lang*
Mädchen in Uniform
Deutschland *Leontine Sagan*
Le Million
France *René Clair*
An American Tragedy
USA *Josef von Sternberg*
City Lights
USA *Charlie Chaplin*
Dracula
USA *Tod Browning*
Frankenstein
USA *James Whale*
Tarzan the Ape Man
USA *W.S. Van Dyke*

1932

Das blaue Licht
Deutschland *Leni Riefenstahl*
L'Affaire est dans le sac
France *Pierre Prévert*
Vampyr
France *Carl Theodor Dreyer*
Boudu sauvé des eaux
France *Jean Renoir*
Blonde Venus
USA *Josef von Sternberg*
Trouble in Paradise
USA *Ernst Lubitsch*
Freaks
USA *Tod Browning*
I am a Fugitive from a Chain Gang
USA *Mervyn LeRoy*
Scarface
USA *Howard Hawks*
Shanghai Express
USA *Josef von Sternberg*

1933

Zéro de conduite
France *Jean Vigo*
L'Atalante
France *Jean Vigo*
Man of Aran
Britain *Robert Flaherty*
The Private Life of Henry VIII
Britain *Alexander Korda*
Duck Soup
USA *Leo McCarey*
The Gold Diggers of 1933
USA *Mervyn LeRoy*
King Kong
USA *M.C. Cooper/E. Schoedsack*
Three Little Pigs
USA *Walt Disney*
Forty-Second Street
USA *Lloyd Bacon*
Queen Christina
USA *Rouben Mamoulian*

1934

Madame Bovary
France *Jean Renoir*
Toni
France *Jean Renoir*
The Man Who Knew Too Much
Britain *Alfred Hitchcock*
Boule de suif
UdSSR *Mikhail Romm*
A Story Of Floating Weeds
Japan *Yasujiro Ozu*
Cleopatra
USA *Cecil B. De Mille*
It Happened One Night
USA *Frank Capra*
Of Human Bondage
USA *John Cromwell*
Our Daily Bread
USA *King Vidor*
A Tale of Two Cities
USA *Jack Conway*

1935

Le Crime de Monsieur Lange
France *Jean Renoir*
Le Dernier Millionaire
France *René Clair*
La Kermesse héroique
France *Jacques Feyder*
Housing Problems
Britain *Edgar Anstey/Arthur Elton*
Song of Ceylon
Britain *Basil Wright*
The Thirty-Nine Steps
Britain *Alfred Hitchcock*
Becky Sharp
USA *Rouben Mamoulian*
The Informer
USA *John Ford*
A Midsummer Night's Dream
USA *Max Reinhardt*
Top Hat
USA *Mark Sandvich*

1936

Triumph des Willens
Deutschland *Leni Riefenstahl*
Les Bas-Fonds
France *Jean Renoir*
César
France *Marcel Pagnol*
The Ghost Goes West
Britain *René Clair*
Rembrandt
Britain *Alexander Korda*
The Secret Agent
Britain *Alfred Hitchcock*
Circus
UdSSR *Grigori Alexandrov*
Fury
USA *Fritz Lang*
Mr Deeds Goes to Town
USA *Frank Capra*
Modern Times
USA *Charlie Chaplin*

1937

La Grande Illusion
France *Jean Renoir*
Pépé le Moko
France *Julien Duvivier*
The Edge of the World
Britain *Michael Powell*
The Elephant Boy
Britain *Robert Flaherty/Zoltan Korda*
Oh, Mr Porter!
Britain *Marcel Varnel*
A Yank at Oxford
Britain *Jack Conway*
The Hurricane
USA *John Ford*
Snow White and the Seven Dwarfs
USA *Walt Disney*
A Star is Born
USA *William Wellman*
You Only Live Once
USA *Fritz Lang*

1938

La Bête humaine
France *Jean Renoir*
La Règle du jeu
France *Jean Renoir*
La Femme du boulanger
France *Marcel Pagnol*
Hôtel du Nord
France *Marcel Carné*
Quai des Brumes
France *Marcel Carné*
The Lady Vanishes
Britain *Alfred Hitchcock*
Alexandr Nevsky
UdSSR *Sergei Eisenstein*
Angels with Dirty Faces
USA *Michael Curtiz*
Boys' Town
USA *Norman Taurog*
Bringing Up Baby
USA *Howard Hawks*

1939

Le Jour se lève
France *Marcel Carné*
The Four Feathers
Britain *Zoltan Korda*
Goodbye, Mr Chips
Britain *Soltan Wood*
Jamaica Inn
Britain *Alfred Hitchcock*
**The Story of the Last
Chrysanthemums**
Japan *Kenji Mizoguchi*
Gone with the Wind
USA *Victor Fleming*
The Hunchback of Notre Dame
USA *William Dieterle*
Ninotchka
USA *Ernst Lubitsch*
Stagecoach
USA *John Ford*
The Wizard of Oz
USA *Victor Fleming*

1940

Jud Süß
Deutschland *Viet Harlan*
Gaslight
Britain *Thorold Dickinson*
London Can Take It!
Britain *Humphrey Jennings/Harry Walt*
Citizen Kane
USA *Orson Welles*
Angels over Broadway
USA *Ben Hecht, Lee Garmes*
Fantasia
USA *Walt Disney*
The Foreign Correspondent
USA *Alfred Hitchcock*
The Great Dictator
USA *Charlie Chaplin*
The Grapes of Wrath
USA *John Ford*
Rebecca
USA *Alfred Hitchcock*

1941

La nave bianca
Italia *Roberto Rossellini*
Teresa Venerdì
Italia *Vittorio De Sica*
The Loyal Forty-Seven Ronin
Japan *Kenji Mozuguchi*
Babies on Broadway
USA *Busby Berkeley*
Hellzapoppin'
USA *H.C. Potter*
The Little Foxes
USA *William Wyler*
The Maltese Falcon
USA *John Huston*
Suspicion
USA *Alfred Hitchcock*
High Sierra
USA *Raoul Walsh*
Tobacco Road
USA *John Ford*

1942

In Which We Serve
Britain *Noel Coward/David Lean*
One of Our Aircraft Is Missing
Britain *Michael Powell/Emeric Pressburger*
Went the Day Well?
Britain *Alberto Cavalcanti*
Bambi
USA *Walt Disney*
Casablanca
USA *Michael Curtiz*
Saboteur
USA *Alfred Hitchcock*
To Be Or Not To Be
USA *Ernst Lubitsch*
Yankee Doodle Dandy
USA *Michael Curtiz*
The Magnificent Ambersons
USA *Orson Welles*
Mrs. Miniver
USA *William Wyler*

1943

Les Anges du péché
France *Robert Bresson*
Le Corbeau
France *Henri-Georges Clouzot*
Ossessione
Italia *Luchino Visconti*
L'uomo della croce
Italia *Roberto Rossellini*
Fires Were Started
Britain *Humphrey Jennings*
The Life and Death of Colonel Blimp
Britain *Michael Powell/Emeric Pressburger*
Day of Wrath
Dänemark *Carl Theodor Dreyer*
Sanshiro Sugata
Japan *Akira Kurosawa*
The Outlaw
USA *Howard Hughes*
The Oxbow Incident
USA *William Wellman*

1944

Fanny by Gaslight
Britain *Anthony Asquith*
The Way Ahead
Britain *Carol Reed*
Henry V
Britain *Laurence Olivier*
Frenzy
Schweden *Alf Sjöberg*
Ivan the Terrible Part 1
UdSSR *Sergei Eisenstein*
Double Indemnity
USA *Billy Wilder*
Hail the Conquering Hero
USA *Preston Sturges*
Meet Me in St Louis
USA *Vincente Minnelli*
The Seventh Cross
USA *Fred Zinnemann*
To Have and Have Not
USA *Howard Hawks*

1945

Les Dames du Bois de Boulogne
France *Robert Bresson*
Les Enfants du paradis
France *Marcel Carné*
Roma città aperta
Italia *Roberto Rossellini*
Blithe Spirit
Britain *David Lean*
Brief Encounter
Britain *David Lean*
A Diary for Timothy
Britain *Humphrey Jennings*
Nicholas Nickleby
Britain *Alberto Cavalcanti*
The Lost Weekend
USA *Billy WIlder*
The Memphis Belle
USA *William Wyler*
The Picture of Dorian Gray
USA *Albert Lewin*

1946

La Belle et la bête
France *Jean Cocteau*
Une Partie de campagne
France *Jean Renoir*
Paisà
Italia *Roberto Rossellini*
Great Expectations
Britain *David Lean*
A Matter of Life and Death
Britain *Michael Powell/Emeric Pressburger*
Ivan the Terrible Part 2
UdSSR *Sergei Eisenstein*
The Best Years of Our Lives
USA *William Wyler*
The Big Sleep
USA *Howard Hawks*
The Diary of a Chambermaid
USA *Jean Renoir*
My Darling Clementine
USA *John Ford*

1947

Jour de fête
France *Jacques Tati*
Germania, anno zero
Italia *Roberto Rossellini*
Black Narcissus
Britain *Michael Powell/Emeric Pressburger*
Duel in the Sun
USA *King Vidor*
The Fugitive
USA *John Ford*
It's a Wonderful Life
USA *Frank Capra*
Monsieur Verdoux
USA *Charlie Chaplin*
Summer Holiday
USA *Rouben Mamoulian*
The Treasure of the Sierra Madre
USA *John Huston*
Crossfire
USA *Edward Dmytryk*

1948

Les Parents terribles
France *Jean Cocteau*
Ladri di biciclette
Italia *Vittorio De Sica*
La terra trema
Italia *Luchino Visconti*
Hamlet
Britain *Laurence Olivier*
The Red Shoes
Britain *Michael Powell/Emeric Pressburger*
Key Largo
USA *John Huston*
The Lady from Shanghai
USA *Orson Welles*
Letter from an Unknown Woman
USA *Max Ophüls*
Louisiana Story
USA *Robert J. Flaherty*
Red River
USA *Howard Hawks*

1949	1950	1951
Le Sang des bêtes	**Les Enfants terribles**	**Le Journal d'un curé de campagne**
France *Georges Franju*	France *Jean-Pierre Melville*	France *Robert Bresson*
Kind Hearts and Coronets	**Orphée**	**Hakuchi**
Britain *Robert Hamer*	France *Jean Cocteau*	Japan *Akira Kurosawa*
Passport to Pimlico	**La Ronde**	**Miss Julie**
Britain *Henry Cornelius*	France *Max Ophüls*	Schweden *Alf Sjöberg*
The Third Man	**Cronaca di un amore**	**The Lavender Hill Mob**
Britain *Carol Reed*	Italia *Michelangelo Antonioni*	Britain *Charles Crichton*
Prison	**The Battle of Stalingrad**	**The Man in the White Suit**
Schweden *Ingmar Bergman*	UdSSR *Vladimir Petrov*	Britain *Alexander Mackendrick*
Adam's Rib	**Rashomon**	**The Tales of Hoffmann**
USA *George Cukor*	Japan *Akira Kurosawa*	Britain *Michael Powell/Emeric Pressburger*
Home of the Brave	**Los Olvidados**	**The African Queen**
USA *Mark Robson*	Mexiko *Luis Buñuel*	USA *John Huston*
On the Town	**The Asphalt Jungle**	**The Red Badge of Courage**
USA *Stanley Donen/Gene Kelly*	USA *John Huston*	USA *John Huston*
She Wore a Yellow Ribbon	**Rio Grande**	**Strangers on a Train**
USA *John Ford*	USA *John Ford*	USA *Alfred Hitchcock*
White Heat	**Sunset Boulevard**	**A Streetcar Named Desire**
USA *Raoul Walsh*	USA *Billy Wilder*	USA *Elia Kazan*

1952

Hôtel des Invalides
France *Georges Franju*
Umberto D
Italia *Vittorio De Sica*
I vinti
Italia *Michelangelo Antonioni*
The Titfield Thunderbolt
Britain *Charles Crichton*
Summer with Monika
Schweden *Ingmar Bergman*
El
Mexiko *Luis Buñuel*
High Noon
USA *Fred Zinneman*
Othello
USA *Orson Welles*
Rancho Notorious
USA *Fritz Lang*
The Big Sky
USA *Howard Hawks*

1953

Les Vacances de M. Hulot
France *Jacques Tati*
Salaire de la peur
France *Henri-Georges Cluzot*
La signora senza camelie
Italia *Michelangelo Antonioni*
I vitelloni
Italia *Federico Fellini*
Sawdust and Tinsel
Schweden *Ingmar Bergman*
Tokyo Story
Japan *Yasujiro Ozu*
Ugetsu Story
Japan *Kenji Mizoguchi*
It Came from Outer Space
USA *Jack Arnold*
Roman Holiday
USA *William Wyler*
The Big Heat
USA *Fritz Lang*

1954

Huis-clos
France *Jacqueline Audry*
Senso
Italia *Luchino Visconti*
La strada
Italia *Federico Fellini*
Ordet
Dänemark *Carl Theodor Dreyer*
A Generation
Poland *Andrzej Wajda*
Seven Samurai
Japan *Akira Kurosawa*
The Caine Mutiny
USA *Edward Dmytryk*
Dial M for Murder
USA *Alfred Hitchcock*
Johnny Guitar
USA *Nicholas Ray*
Seven Brides for Seven Brothers
USA *Stanley Donen*

1955	1956	1957

Le amiche
Italia *Michelangelo Antonioni*
The Ladykillers
Britain *Alexander Mackendrick*
Smiles of the Summer Night
Schweden *Ingmar Bergman*
Pather Panchali
India *Satyajit Ray*
The Blackboard Jungle
USA *Richard Brooks*
East of Eden
USA *Elia Kazan*
Kiss Me Deadly
USA *Robert Aldrich*
The Man from Laramie
USA *Anthony Mann*
The Night of the Hunter
USA *Charles Laughton*
Rebel Without a Cause
USA *Nicholas Ray*

Nuit et brouillard
France *Alain Resnais*
Richard III
Britain *Laurence Olivier*
The Seventh Seal
Schweden *Ingmar Berman*
The Burmese Harp
Japan *Kon Ichikawa*
Baby Doll
USA *Elia Kazan*
The Killing
USA *Stanley Kubrick*
Moby Dick
USA *John Huston*
The Searchers
USA *John Ford*
The Ten Commandments
USA *Cecil B. De Mille*
The Trouble with Harry
USA *Alfred Hitchcock*

Ascenseur pour l'échafaud
France *Louis Malle*
Il grido
Italia *Michelangelo Antonioni*
A King in New York
Britain *Charlie Chaplin*
Kanal
Poland *Andrzej Wajda*
Wild Strawberries
Schweden *Ingmar Bergman*
The Lower Depths
Japan *Akira Kurosawa*
Throne of Blood
Japan *Akira Kurosawa*
Jailhouse Rock
USA *Richard Thorpe*
Paths of Glory
USA *Stanley Kubrick*
A King in New York
USA *Charlie Chaplin*

1958	1959	1960
Les Amants	**Hiroshima mon amour**	**Tirez sur le pianiste**
France *Louis Malle*	France *Alain Resnais*	France *François Truffaut*
Paris nous appartient	**Les quatre cent coups**	**Le Petit Soldat**
France *Jacques Rivette*	France *François Truffaut*	France *Jean-Luc Godard*
The Bridge on the River Kwai	**A bout de souffle**	**Le Testament d'Orphée**
Britain *David Lean*	France *Jean-Luc Godard*	France *Jean Cocteau*
We Are the Lambeth Boys	**Les Yeux sans visage**	**Zazie dans le Métro**
Britain *Karel Reisz*	France *Georges Franju*	France *Louis Malle*
Ashes and Diamonds	**Dorp aan de rivier**	**La dolce vita**
Poland *Andrzej Wajda*	Nederlands *Fons Rademakers*	Italia *Federico Fellini*
Two Men and a Wardrobe	**Peeping Tom**	**Rocco e i suoi fratelli**
Poland *Roman Polanski*	Britain *Michael Powell*	Italia *Luchino Visconti*
The Hidden Fortress	**The Virgin Spring**	**L'avventura**
Japan *Akira Kurosawa*	Schweden *Ingmar Bergman*	Italia *Michelangelo Antonioni*
Nazarin	**Apur Sansar**	**Saturday Night and Sunday Morning**
Mexiko *Luis Buñuel*	India *Satyajit Ray*	Britain *Karel Reisz*
A Touch of Evil	**Some Like It Hot**	**The Apartment**
USA *Orson Welles*	USA *Billy WIlder*	USA *Billy Wilder*
Vertigo	**Shadows**	**Psycho**
USA *Alfred Hitchcock*	USA *John Cassavetes*	USA *Alfred Hitchcock*

1961	1962	1963
Jules et Jim France *François Truffaut*	**Le Caporal épinglé** France *Alain Resnais*	**Les Carabiniers** France *Jean-Luc Godard*
Cléo de 5 à 7 France *Agnès Varda*	**Vivre sa vie** France *Jean-Luc Godard*	**Le Feu follet** France *Louis Malle*
Cuba, si! France *Chris Marker*	**L'eclisse** Italia *Michelangelo Antonioni*	**La Jetée** France *Chris Marker*
Une Femme est une femme France *Jean-Luc Godard*	**Lolita** Britain *Stanley Kubrick*	**Muriel, ou le temps d'un retour** France *Alain Resnais*
L'Année dernière à Marienbad France *Alain Resnais*	**The Loneliness of the Long-Distance Runner** Britain *Tony Richardson*	**Il gattopardo** Italia *Luchino Visconti*
Accattone Italia *Pier Paolo Pasolini*	**El angel exterminador** España *Luis Buñuel*	**8½** Italia *Federico Fellini*
La notte Italia *Michelangelo Antonioni*	**Knife in the Water** Poland *Roman Polanski*	**The Silence** Schweden *Ingmar Bergman*
Il posto Italia *Ermanno Olmi*	**The Manchurian Candidate** USA *John Frankenheimer*	**Alone in the Pacific** Japan *Kon Ichikawa*
Viridiana España *Luis Buñuel*	**What Ever Happened to Baby Jane?** USA *Robert Aldrich*	**The Balcony** USA *Joseph Strick*
Through a Glass Darkly Schweden *Ingmar Bergman*	**The Man Who Shot Liberty Valance** USA *John Ford*	**The Birds** USA *Alfred Hitchcock*

1964	1965	1966
Bande à part	**Alphaville**	**Au Hasard, Balthazar**
France *Jean-Luc Godard*	France *Jean-Luc Godard*	France *Robert Bresson*
Le Journal d'une femme de chambre	**Pierrot le fou**	**Belle de Jour**
France *Luis Buñuel*	France *Jean-Luc Godard*	France *Luis Buñuel*
Les Parapluies de Cherbourg	**Giulietta degli spiriti**	**La Guerre est finie**
France *Jacques Demy*	Italia *Federico Fellini*	France *Alain Resnais*
Prima della revoluzione	**I pugni in tasca**	**Un Homme et une femme**
Italia *Bernardo Bertolucci*	Italia *Merco Bellocchio*	France *Claude Lelouch*
Per un pugno di dollari	**Cul-de-sac**	**La battaglia di Algeri**
Italia *Sergio Leone*	Britain *Roman Polanski*	Italia *Gillo Pontecorvo*
Il vangelo secondo Matteo	**Darling**	**Uccellacci e uccellini**
Italia *Pier Paolo Pasolini*	Britain *John Schlesinger*	Italia *Pier Paolo Pasolini*
Gertrude	**The War Game**	**Campañadas a medianoche (Falstaff)**
Dänemark *Carl Theodor Dreyer*	Britain *Peter Watkins*	España *Orson Welles*
Shakespeare Wallah	**A Blonde in Love**	**Blow-Up**
India *James Ivory*	Tschechoslowake *Milós Forman*	Britain *Michelangelo Antonioni*
Onibaba	**Red Beard**	**Closely Observed Trains**
Japan *Kaneto Shindo*	Japan *Akira Kurosawa*	Tschechoslowake *Jiři Menzel*
Woman of the Dunes	**Simon nel desierto**	**Who's Afraid of Virginia Woolf?**
Japan *Hiroshi Teshigahara*	Mexiko *Luis Buñuel*	USA *Mike Nichols*

1967

Trans-Europ-Express
France *Alain Robbe-Grillet*
Weekend
France *Jean-Luc Godard*
Il buono, il brutto, il cattivo
Italia *Sergio Leone*
Elvira Madigan
Schweden *Bo Widerberg*
I am Curious – Yellow
Schweden *Vilgot Sjöman*
Andrei Rublev
UdSSR *Andrei Tarkovsky*
The Fireman's Ball
Tschechoslowake *Milós Forman*
The Dirty Dozen
USA *Robert Aldrich*
Guess Who's Coming to Dinner
USA *Stanley Kramer*
Point Blank
USA *John Boorman*

1968

Chronik der Anna Magdalena Bach
BRD *Jean-Marie Straub*
Teorema
Italia *Pier Paolo Pasolini*
The Charge of the Light Brigade
Britain *Tony Richardson*
If
Britain *Lindsay Anderson*
The Doll
Poland *Wojciech Jerzy Has*
The Hour of the Wolf
Schweden *Ingmar Bergman*
2001: A Space Odyssey
USA *Stanley Kubrick*
The Graduate
USA *Mike Nichols*
Rosemary's Baby
USA *Roman Polanski*
The Thomas Crown Affair
USA *Thomas Jewison*

1969

Le Chagrin et la pitié
France *Marcel Ophüls*
Z
France *Costa-Gavras*
Satyricon
Italia *Federico Fellini*
C'era una volta il West
Italia *Sergio Leone*
The Yellow Submarine
Britain *George Dunning*
Adalen 31
Schweden *Bo Widerberg*
Shinjuku dorobo nikki
Japan *Nagisa Oshima*
Easy Rider
USA *Dennis Hopper*
The Wild Bunch
USA *Sam Peckinpah*
Zabriskie Point
USA *Michelangelo Antonioni*

1970

Deep End
BRD *Jerzy Skolimowski*
L'Enfant sauvage
France *François Truffaut*
Il conformista
Italia *Bernardo Bertolucci*
Medea
Italia *Pier Paolo Pasolini*
La strategia del ragno
Italia *Bernardo Bertolucci*
Performance
Britain *Nicholas Roeg*
Catch 22
USA *Mike Nichols*
Five Easy Pieces
USA *Bob Rafelson*
Husbands
USA *John Cassavetes*
MASH
USA *Robert Altman*

1971

Blanche
France *Walerian Borowczyk*
Morte a Venezia
Italia *Luchino Visconti*
Decamerone
Italia *Pier Paolo Pasolini*
A Clockwork Orange
Britain *Stanley Kubrick*
The Devils
Britain *Ken Russell*
Straw Dogs
Britain *Sam Peckinpah*
Sunday, Bloody Sunday
Britain *John Schlesinger*
Joe Hill
Schweden *Bo Widerberg*
Walkabout
Australia *Nicholas Roeg*
The French Connection
USA *William Friedkin*

1972

Aguirre, der Zorn Gottes
BRD *Werner Herzog*
Die bitteren Tränen der Petra von Kant
BRD *Rainer Werner Fassbinder*
Die Angst des Tormanns beim Elfmeter
BRD *Wim Wenders*
Le Charme discret de la bourgeoisie
France *Luis Buñuel*
I raconti di Canterbury
Italia *Pier Paolo Pasolini*
Ultimo tango a Parigi
Italia *Bernardo Bertolucci*
Macbeth
Britain *Roman Polanski*
My Childhood
Britain *Bill Douglas*
O Lucky Man!
Britain *Lindsay Anderson*

1973

Angst essen Seele auf
BRD *Rainer Werner Fassbinder*
La Grande Bouffe
France *Marco Ferreri*
La Nuite americaine
France *François Truffaut*
Themroc
France *Claude Faraldo*
Amarcord
Italia *Federico Fellini*
Portiere di notte
Italia *Liliana Cavani*
El espiritu de la colamena
España *Victor Erice*
Scenes from a Marriage
Schweden *Ingmar Bergman*
Don't Look Now
Britain *Nicholas Roeg*
The Sting
USA *George Roy Hill*

1974

Effi Briest
BRD *Rainer Werner Fassbinder*
Jeder für sich und Gott gegen alle
BRD *Werner Herzog*
Céline et Julie vont en bateau
France *Jacques Rivette*
Lancelot du Lac
France *Robert Bresson*
Stavisky
France *Alain Resnais*
The Mirror
UdSSR *Andrei Tarkovsky*
The Cars that Ate Paris
Australia *Peter Weir*
Alice Doesn't Live Here Anymore
USA *Martin Scorsese*
Blazing Saddles
USA *Mel Brooks*
Chinatown
USA *Roman Polanski*

1975

F for Fake
France *Orson Welles*
L'Histoire d'O
France *Just Jaeckın*
Professione: Reporter
Italia *Michelangelo Antonioni*
Salò
Italia *Pier Paolo Pasolini*
Barry Lyndon
Britain *Stanley Kubrick*
Monty Python and the Holy Grail
Britain *Terry Gilliam/Terry Jones*
Dersu Uzala
Japan *Akira Kurosawa*
Picnic at Hanging Rock
Australia *Peter Weir*
The French Connection 2
USA *John Frankenheimer*
One Flew Over the Cuckoo's Nest
USA *Milós Forman*

1976

Herz aus Glas
BRD *Werner Herzog*
Im Lauf der Zeit
BRD *Wim Wenders*
Die Marquise von O. . .
BRD *Eric Rohmer*
Noirs et blancs en couleurs
France *Jean-Jacques Annaud*
1900
Italia *Bernardo Bertolucci*
The Man Who Fell to Earth
Britain *Nicholas Roeg*
Ai No Corrida
Japan *Nagisa Oshima*
Assault on Precinct 13
USA *John Carpenter*
The Missouri Breaks
USA *Arthur Penn*
Taxi Driver
USA *Martin Scorsese*

1977

Der amerikanische Freund
BRD *Wim Wenders*
Cet Obscur Objet du désir
France *Luis Buñuel*
Le Diable, probablement
France *Robert Bresson*
Providence
France *Alain Resnais*
Padre Padrone
Italia *Paolo/Vittorio Taviani*
L'albero degli zoccoli
Italia *Ermanno Olmi*
The Jabberwocky
Britain *Terry Gilliam*
Eraserhead
Britain *David Lynch*
Man of Marble
Poland *Andrzej Wajda*
Blood Wedding
Marokko *Souhel Ben Barka*

1978

In einem Jahr mit 13 Monden
BRD *Rainer Werner Fassbinder*
Perceval le Gallois
France *Eric Rohmer*
Violette Nozière
France *Claude Chabrol*
Superman
Britain *Richard Donner*
Hungarian Rhapsody
Ungarn *Miklós Jancsó*
Ai no borei
Japan *Nagisa Oshima*
The Chant of Jimmy Blacksmith
Australia *Fred Schepisi*
Blue Collar
USA *Paul Schrader*
The Deer Hunter
USA *Michael Cimono*
A Wedding
USA *Robert Altman*

1979

Die Ehe der Maria Braun
BRD *Rainer Werner Fassbinder*
Nosferatu – Phantom der Nacht
BRD *Werner Herzog*
Die Blechtrommel
BRD *Volker Schlöndorff*
Woyzeck
BRD *Werner Herzog*
La città delle donne
Italia *Federico Fellini*
Don Giovanni
Italia *Joseph Losey*
La luna
Italia *Bernardo Bertolucci*
Mad Max
Australia *George Miller*
My Brilliant Career
Australia *Gillian Armstrong*
Apocalypse Now
USA *Francis Ford Coppola*

1980

Berlin-Alexanderplatz
BRD *Rainer Werner Fassbinder*
Mon Oncle d'Amérique
France *Alain Resnais*
Diva
France *Jean-Jacques Beineix*
The Conductor
Poland *Andrzej Wajda*
'Breaker' Morant
Australia *Bruce Beresford*
The Shining
USA *Stanley Kubrick*
Raging Bull
USA *Martin Scorsese*
Heaven's Gate
USA *Michael Cimino*
Atlantic City
Canada *Louis Malle*
Scanners
Canada *David Cronenberg*

1981

Lola
BRD *Rainer Werner Fassbinder*
The French Lieutenant's Woman
Britain *Karel Reisz*
Chariots of Fire
Britain *Hugh Hudson*
Pixote
Portugal *Hector Babenco*
Mephisto
Ungarn *István Szabó*
The Raiders of the Lost Ark
USA *Steven Spielberg*
Reds
USA *Warren Beatty*
My Dinner with André
USA *Louis Malle*
Excalibur
USA *John Boorman*
The Postman Always Rings Twice
USA *Bob Rafelson*

1982

Fitzcarraldo
BRD *Werner Herzog*
Querelle
BRD *Rainer Werner Fassbinder*
La notte di San Lorenzo
Italia *Paolo/Vittorio Taviani*
Moonlighting
Britain *Jerzy Skolimowski*
Fanny and Alexander
Schweden *Ingmar Bergman*
Yol
Türkei *Yilmaz Güney/Serif Gören*
Blade Runner
USA *Ridley Scott*
Tootsie
USA *Sydney Pollack*
E. T.
USA *Steven Spielberg*
Sophie's Choice
USA *Alan J. Pakula*

1983

Pauline à la plage
France *Eric Rohmer*
Danton
France *Andrzej Wajda*
Merry Christmas, Mr Lawrence
Britain *Nagisa Oshima*
Monty Python's The Meaning of Life
Britain *Terry Jones*
Educating Rita
Britain *Lewis Gilbert*
The Ballad of Narayama
Japan *Shohei Imamura*
Rumblefish
USA *Francis Ford Coppola*
Outsiders
USA *Francis Ford Coppola*
Scarface
USA *Brian De Palma*
Zelig
USA *Woody Allen*

1984

Heimat
BRD *Edgar Reitz*
L'Amour à mort
France *Alain Resnais*
Home and the World
India *Satyajit Ray*
The Yellow Earth
China *Kaige Chen*
Broadway Danny Rose
USA *Woody Allen*
Paris, Texas
USA *Wim Wenders*
The Terminator
USA *James Cameron*
Dune
USA *David Lynch*
The Cotton Club
USA *Francis Ford Coppola*
Amadeus
USA *Milós Forman*

1985

Subway
France *Luc Besson*
Brazil
Britain *Terry Gilliam*
When Father was Away on Business
Yugoslavia *Emir Kusturica*
Colonel Redl
Ungarn *István Szabó*
Ran
Japan *Akira Kurosawa*
Kiss of the Spider Woman
Brazil *Hector Babenco*
Back to the Future
USA *Robert Zemeckis*
Desperately Seeking Susan
USA *Susan Seidelman*
Silverado
USA *Lawrence Kasdan*
Mishima
USA *Paul Schrader*

1986

Betty Blue
France *Jean-Jacques Beineix*
Ginger e Fred
Italia *Federico Fellini*
Sid and Nancy
Britain *Alex Cox*
The Bee-keepers
Griechenland *Theo Angelopoulos*
My Life as a Dog
Schweden *Lasse Hallström*
Sacrifice
UdSSR *Andrei Tarkovsky*
Horse Thief
China *Tian Zhuangzhuang*
Blue Velvet
USA *David Lynch*
Hannah and her SIsters
USA *Woody Allen*
Aliens
USA *James Cameron*

1987	1988	1989
Mauvais Sang France *Léos Carax*	**Himmel über Berlin** BRD *Wim Wenders*	**Monsieur Hire** France *Patrice Leconte*
La ley del deseo España *Pedro Almodovar*	**Mujeres al bordo de un ataque de nervios** España *Pedro Almodovar*	**My Left Foot** Britain *Jim Sheridan*
The Last Emperor China *Bernardo Bertolucci*	**A World Apart** Britain *Chris Menges*	**Sweetie** Australia *Jane Campion*
Red Sorghum China *Zhang Yimou*	**Pelle the Conqueror** Schweden *Bille August*	**Batman** USA *Tim Burton*
Radio Days USA *Woody Allen*	**The Cannibals** Portugal *Manoel de Oliveira*	**sex, lies and videotape** USA *Stephen Soderbergh*
The Untouchables USA *Brian De Palma*	**Beetlejuice** USA *Tim Burton*	**Driving Miss Daisy** USA *Bruce Beresford*
Full Metal Jacket USA *Stanley Kubrick*	**Who Framed Roger Rabbit?** USA *Robert Zemeckis*	**Do the Right Thing** USA *Spike Lee*
The Dead USA *John Huston*	**Dangerous Liaisons** USA *Stephen Frears*	**Dead Poets' Society** USA *Peter Weir*
The Witches of Eastwick USA *George Miller*	**The Last Temptation of Christ** USA *Martin Scorsese*	**Crimes and Misdemeanours** USA *Woody Allen*
The Empire of the Sun USA *Steven Spielberg*	**The Rain Man** USA *Barry Levinson*	**Mystery Train** USA *Jim Jarmusch*

1990

Cyrano de Bergerac
France *Jean-Paul Rappeneau*
Riff-Raff
Britain *Ken Loach*
Akira Kurosawa's Dreams
Japan *Akira Kurosawa*
Wild at Heart
USA *David Lynch*
Dances with Wolves
USA *Kevin Costner*
Goodfellas
USA *Martin Scorsese*
Pretty Woman
USA *Garry Marshall*
Teenage Mutant Ninja Turtles
USA *Steve Barron*
Edward Scissorhands
USA *Tim Burton*
Dick Tracy
USA *Warren Beatty*

1991

La Double Vie de Véronique
France *Krzysztof Kieslówski*
Les Amants du Pont Neuf
France *Léos Carax*
Tous les matins du monde
France *Alain Corneau*
Van Gogh
France *Maurice Pialat*
Truly, Madly, Deeply
Britain *Anthony Minghella*
Raise the Red Lantern
China *Zhang Yimou*
The Silence of the Lambs
USA *Jonathan Demme*
Reservoir Dogs
USA *Quentin Tarantino*
Thelma and Louise
USA *Ridley Scott*
JFK
USA *Oliver Stone*

1992

Orlando
Britain *Sally Potter*
The Crying Game
Britain *Neil Jordan*
Strictly Ballroom
Australia *Baz Luhrmann*
Basic Instinct
USA *Paul Verhoeven*
Dracula
USA *Francis Ford Coppola*
The Last of the Mohicans
USA *Michael Mann*
A River Runs Through It
USA *Robert Redford*
Husbands and Wives
USA *Woody Allen*
The Player
USA *Robert Altman*
Malcolm X
USA *Spike Lee*

1993	1994
Smoking No Smoking France *Alain Resnais*	**La Reine Margot** France *Patrice Chéreau*
Trois Couleurs: Bleu France *Krzysztof Kieslówski*	**Caro diario** Italia *Nanni Moretti*
Naked Britain *Mike Leigh*	**Four Weddings and a Funeral** Britain *Mike Newell*
The Piano Australia *Jane Campion*	**Muriel's Wedding** Australia *P.J. Hogan*
Farewell My Concubine China *Chen Kaige*	**Eat Drink Man Woman** Taiwan *Ang Lee*
Como agua para chocolate Mexiko *Alfonso Arau*	**Forest Gump** USA *Robert Zemeckis*
Schindler's List USA *Steven Spielberg*	**Natural Born Killers** USA *Oliver Stone*
Philadelphia USA *Jonathan Demme*	**Pulp Fiction** USA *Quentin Tarantino*
Short Cuts USA *Robert Altman*	**Bullets over Broadway** USA *Woody Allen*
32 Short Films about Glenn Gould Canada *François Girard*	**Exotica** Canada *Atom Egoyan*

1995

Trois Couleurs: Rouge
France *Krzysztof Kieslówski*
Death and the Maiden
France *Roman Polanski*
Land and Freedom
Britain *Ken Loach*
The Madness of King George
Britain *Nicholas Hytner*
Shallow Grave
Britain *Danny Boyle*
Burnt by the Sun
Rußland *Nikita Mikhalkov*
To Live
China *Zhang Yimou*
The Usual Suspects
USA *Bryan Singer*
Braveheart
USA *Mel Gibson*
Speed
USA *Jan De Bont*

Acknowledgements
Music in the Marstall: Patrick Mimran
Actor in the Marstall: Jason Phipps
Loans to the Marstall exhibition:
Deutsches Museum Munich, thanks to Prof.
Dr. Wolf Peter Fehlhammer, Dr. Cornelia
Kemp;
Münchner Stadtmuseum, thanks to Dr.
Wolfgang Till, Dr. Thomas Weidner
Film lists: David Robinson/*Sight and Sound*
Year-number design: Constance de Vos
Costumes: Antje Lau
Costume Assistants: Barbara Wagner, Hedy
Benzenhöfer
Properties: Günther Wellner
Properties Assistant: Stefan Reti
Wardrobe: Hans-Ernst Meyer
Masks: Berta Engelhardt-Rieger
Lighting Assistants: Dirk Nijland, Anthoni
R.D. Fielmich jr
Marstall Lighting Assistants: Florian
Schröter, Sandro Tondat
Marstall Sound Assistant: Alexander Jessen

Dank
Musik im Marstall: Patrick Mimran
Darsteller im Marstall: Jason Phipps
Leihgaben:
Deutsches Museum München, Danksagung
an Prof. Dr. Wolf Peter Fehlhammer, Dr.
Cornelia Kemp;
Münchner Stadtmuseum, Danksagung an Dr.
Wolfgang Till, Dr. Thomas Weidner
Film Lists: David Robinson/*Sight and Sound*
Jahreszahlendesign: Constance de Vos
Leiterin Kostüm: Antje Lau
Mitarbeiter Kostüm: Barbara Wagner, Hedy
Benzenhöfer
Leiter Requisite: Günther Wellner
Assistenz Requisite: Stefan Reti
Leitung Garderobe: Hans-Ernst Meyer
Maske: Berta Engelhardt-Rieger
Assistenz Beleuchtung: Dirk Nijland, Anthoni
R.D. Fielmich jr
Assistenz Beleuchtung/Marstall: Florian
Schröter, Sandro Tondat
Assistenz Ton/Marstall: Alexander Jessen